PENGUIN BOOKS

675

HASSAN

BY JAMES ELROY FLECKER

D1314097

PENGUIN
BOOKS

HASSAN

JAMES ELROY
FLECKER

COMPLETE UNABRIDGED

One shilling and sixpence

ABOUT THIS BOOK

Haroun al Raschid, Caliph of Bagdad, was in the habit of
wandering about his city after dark, in search of novelty
and adventure. On one such escapade he was extricated
from a perilous situation by Hassan, a confectioner by
trade but an artist by temperament. As a reward for this
service Hassan, the poor tradesman, was made the Caliph's
favourite and endowed with all the riches and splendour of
the Court. But soon he was made to witness one of those
refinements of cruelty which only an Eastern despot could
evolve to revenge himself upon a woman who was steadfast
in love. Pervaneh the beautiful maiden and Rafi the war-
rior, both captives of the Caliph, chose death together
rather than separation – and Hassan, for denouncing this
infamous judgment, was stripped of his fortune and compelled to witness the horrible execution of the sentence.
Revolted by these infamies Hassan and his friend, Ishak the
poet determined to leave Bagdad and its decadence, and
to find peace by making the pilgrimage of 'The Golden
Road to Samarkand'.

This is the story, based upon some old Turkish tales,
which James Elroy Flecker dramatised when he was working in the Middle East in 1911. It has proved one of the
most spectacular plays to be seen on the modern English
stage, and has been broadcast with equal success. Those
who now read it for the first time in this Penguin edition
will discover that, on the printed page as well, *Hassan* is a
vivid evocation of the traditional splendours and enormi-
ties of ancient Bagdad.

HASSAN

THE STORY OF HASSAN OF BAGDAD

AND HOW HE CAME TO MAKE

THE GOLDEN JOURNEY TO SAMARKAND

A PLAY IN FIVE ACTS

BY JAMES ELROY FLECKER

★

PENGUIN BOOKS

IN ASSOCIATION WITH

WILLIAM HEINEMANN LTD

FIRST PUBLISHED 1922
PUBLISHED IN PENGUIN BOOKS 1948

MADE AND PRINTED IN GREAT BRITAIN
FOR PENGUIN BOOKS LIMITED, HARMONDSWORTH,
BY HUNT, BARNARD AND CO., LTD.,
LONDON AND AYLESBURY

CHARACTERS

HASSAN, a Confectioner
THE CALIPH HAROUN AR RASCHID
ISHAK, his Minstrel
JAFAR, his Vizier
MASRUR, his Executioner
RAFI, King of the Beggars
SELIM, a Friend of Hassan's
THE CAPTAIN OF THE MILITARY
THE CHIEF OF THE POLICE
ALI ⎱
ABDU ⎰ Nondescripts
ALDER ⎫
WILLOW ⎬ Slaves
TAMARISK ⎭
THE PORTER of Yasmin's House
THE CHINESE PHILOSOPHER
A DERVISH
THE FOUNTAIN GHOST
A HERALD
THE PRISON GUARDS
PERVANEH
YASMIN

An AMBASSADOR, a WRESTLER, a CALLIGRAPHIST, a JESTER, GHOSTS, MUTES, DANCING WOMEN, BEGGARS, SOLDIERS, POLICE, ATTENDANTS and CASUAL LOITERERS.

This play, arranged for the stage and produced by Basil Dean, with music by Frederick Delius, scene and costume designs by George W. Harris and Ballets by Michael Fokine, was presented on Thursday, September 20th, 1923, at His Majesty's Theatre, London, by George Grossmith and J. A. E. Malone, by arrangement with Reandean.

INTRODUCTION
(1922)

JAMES ELROY FLECKER was born on November 5th, 1884, the eldest child of the Rev. W. H. Flecker, D.D., later Headmaster of Dean Close School, Cheltenham. He was educated there first and then at Uppingham, then at Trinity College, Oxford, and then at Caius College, Cambridge, where he studied Oriental Languages, with a view to entering the Consular Service. He passed in, was posted to Constantinople (where he first became ill) in 1910, returned to an English sanatorium, was transferred to Smyrna and, in May 1911, married Miss Helle Skiaderessi, a Greek lady. After three months holiday in Corfu, he was sent to Beirut. In March 1913 he fell ill again, and went to Switzerland, there on January 3rd, 1915, to die at Davos. He had published four books of poems and four books in prose. His most important work, the play *Hassan*, he did not live to see either in print or on the stage.

When *Hassan*, nearly eight years after its author's death, was published, it was generally agreed that Flecker's friends had not exaggerated its merits as a stage-play. The one reservation which some of the critics made was that the latter part of it might be found in the theatre unbearably painful. *Hassan* began as a farce, and the development of Flecker's first idea into the play as we have it is interesting in itself and also as an example of the strange processes that go on in the minds of artists, and, above all, perhaps, in the minds of artists who are writing for the stage.

7

The origin of the play was as follows. On entering the Consular Service, Flecker went first to Constantinople and then to Beirut in Syria. From June to August 1911, he spent three months' leave in Corfu, where he occupied himself chiefly in working for the consular examination in Turkish. He was in good health and his spirits were light; the scenery was beautiful and life seemed easy. He wrote a good deal. 'In the cóttage where we lived,' writes Mrs. Flecker, 'he used to spend long hours in the garden beneath a tall orange-tree, sitting in a deep armchair, certainly a relic of the English occupation, watching, pen in hand, a small wood-worm, a little brown-hooded hermit that lived in the arm of the chair, come out of his den and set to pierce a new hole with his saw-beak.' The poems he wrote there included *Yasmin, Saadabad, The Hammam Name, The Golden Journey, In Phaeacia*, and *Oak and Olive*. Amongst the Turkish books he read was a small volume of farcical plays. One of these he translated. It related the adventures of one Hassan, a simple and credulous man, whose friends amused themselves by playing practical jokes upon him with the aid of a Hebrew magician. The magician struck Flecker's fancy, and he sketched a short farce in which Zachariah the Jew and his philtres were the centre of interest. The manuscript no longer exists. The manner of it may be deduced from the opening of *Hassan*. Flecker had been reading with great delight Dr Mardrus's French translation of the *Arabian Nights*: the lines inscribed on the title page are an example of Mardrus's direct style and of the spirit in which Flecker conceived his comedy. There was a woman in the farce named Yasmin; and soon after he had written this little play he wrote, 'Yasmin: a Ghazel', the lovely song which now appears in *Hassan* but which was originally composed

8

without any reference to a dramatic setting. The name had suggested the song, the song suggested a play: for Flecker next thought of writing a three-act comedy in which Yasmin was to be the chief feminine character. About the same time he wrote, 'A Diwan of the West', the poem published later under the title 'Prologue', in which the Golden Journey to Samarkand first appears. In July this three-act comedy was sent to London to be typed, and the first act of the draft is before me as I write. It is covered with scrawls, for it became the basis of the ultimate play; and on the title page the words, 'A comedy in Three Acts', are scratched out and 'A play in Five Acts' substituted, the same substitution being made for 'A Farce' on the next page. Here is the whole of this second title page as it originally stood.

THE STORY OF HASSAN OF BAGDAD
AND HOW HE CAME TO MAKE THE GOLDEN JOURNEY TO SAMARKAND

A Farce

'And he laughed so, he fell back upon his bottom.' (*Arabian Nights*).

'He was seized with inextinguishable laughter.' (English translation of the same.)

THE CALIPH HAROUN AL RASCHID
JAFAR, his Vizier
MASRUR, his Executioner
ISHAK, his Singer and Companion
HASSAN, a Confectioner
SELIM, a Friend of his
YAKUB, a Friend of his
ZACHARIAH, a Jew Magician

9

TULIP, a Negro Boy
YASMIN, a widow Woman
SPLENDOUR, a Lady
SUGAR CANE,
PALM-BRANCH,   } her Maids
MYRTLE BLOSSOM,

Some of these characters disappeared before the final
version was reached: Rafi and Pervaneh, around whose
story the later play was to centre, are not here. The setting
for the first scene was as it stands. Much of the original
dialogue has been retained. The play opened as at present,
but the conversation was between Hassan and Yakub, 'his
friend, stubbly beard, about same age, similar costume'.
Selim came in later; the final play gives Selim all Yakub's
remarks as well as his own, one 'friend' serving instead of
two friends.

Zachariah the Jew, in the play as we have it, never appears on the stage: Selim merely recounts his feats and goes
off to get a philtre from him. In the original comedy Selim
fetches Zachariah, 'a tall bearded individual in a flowing
gown embroidered with signs of the Zodiac and a square
hat'. The Jew asks an outrageous price for his potion;
Hassan cannot pay it:

HASSAN: Woe is me. For if I sold all my possessions, my
   shop and my bed and my carpet and my new sugar
   boiler, that boileth swiftly, I could not amass one-
   fiftieth of that sum. Is there no help, O Master, for the
   children of the poor?

SELIM: O Venerable Zachariah, let me plead for my
   friend, for is it not written:

> Do not shut the cupboard door:
> Give your pieces to the poor,
> Give them generously, or.

When you lost your little store
You may bitterly deplore
That you shut that cupboard door.

ZACHARIAH: My son, the honey of your eloquence has sweetened the acrimony of your resolution. O born under an unhappy star, listen. For twenty pieces of gold, for twenty pieces only I will brew thy mistress a potion of black magic that shall bring her running to thy bed: and there, and thereupon thou shalt know the three delights of Paradise, which are, Approach, Fulfilment and Renewal.

SELIM (*to* HASSAN): His mercy streams towards you like the splendour of the morning. Give Allah the praise, my son, and me the credit and him the Dinars.

HASSAN: Eywallah! Twenty dinars.

SELIM (*in scorn*): Eywallah! Twenty Dinars! Twenty dinars from the Prince of Passion! The price of a small cow for the love of Leila.

HASSAN: Eywallah! Twenty dinars is a monster sum for a very poor man. Complete your generosity, O master of miracles, and turn not my day to darkness for that which for you is a little and for me a lot.

ZACHARIAH: Twenty dinars, O parer of nutmegs, dost thou imagine I desire thy twenty dinars? They would not pay me for the bottle. But it is a law of magic that the philtre will not work for him who makes no sacrifice.

Hassan is sobered, declines to make the purchase and expresses doubts about the efficacy of the remedy. 'Beware, Hassan,' remarks Selim, 'he may change thee into an ass and beat you round the city.' Zachariah retires in dignity and telling Selim to bring Hassan to his house next day, when 'by the God of Jacob I will make him fall flat on his belly in amazement and stupefaction ... I dine with the

Caliph, Farewell.' Yasmin knocks at the door as in the present text, and the rest of the act has been little altered.

No more survives. During his sojourn in Syria, Flecker often thought of turning the rather crude comedy into something more elaborate. Apart from everything else, the old light fantasia was no longer to his mood. The burning sky of the East threw everything into hard relief; the human world around him was pitilessly real, his nerves were on edge and he felt estranged. His health broke down; he went to the Hotel Belvedere at Leysin; and there, in enforced leisure, he took up *Hassan* again with extraordinary energy and passion. The play as we have it, in fact, was composed amid the horrors of Alpine health-resorts, where hundreds of invalids are crowded together in hideous buildings under a glare as crude as that of the East. It expressed a mood which was engendered by cruel realities. In *Hassan* Flecker found an outlet for his thoughts; a refuge he sometimes found in the pure and tranquil beauty of his lyrics of this period, such as *The Blue Noon* and *The Old Ships*. In four or five weeks of July and August 1913, the play was completely remodelled, and most of what we now possess was written, and the 'Golden Journey' was appended as epilogue. In the earlier play there had been a bare mention of a slave-girl Leila who had been stolen from the King of the Beggars for the Caliph's harem. Flecker's imagination fastened on this girl, and this episode, no doubt lightly invented in the beginning: and there came into being all the story of Rafi and Pervaneh, and in that story an image of the immense cruelty and courage and beauty of life, a tragic vision that demanded and indeed compelled all the deepest sincerity of the poet's nature for its embodiment. When the play was finished it was seen by one or two actor-managers and

ultimately reached Mr Basil Dean, then sub-director to
Beerbohm Tree at His Majesty's. Mr Dean asked Flecker
to shorten it for the stage. The request found Flecker and
his wife at Montana, above the Rhone valley. The poet
had a bad relapse at Christmas 1913, and spent nearly
three months in bed, during which time he cut down his
text with unsparing bravery. In March 1914 he went to
Locarno and in May to Davos, where the work of revision
was proceeded with and a scenario written, embodying
various changes for the stage version.

Towards the end of 1914, after the outbreak of the war,
he received from Mr Dean a proposed stage-version. He
was reassured to find that several of his cuts had been rein-
stated and especially delighted that the ghost-scene, which
he had feared no producer would tolerate, was thought
possible. In detail he was able to examine the first act only;
but he was pleased at the respectful handling of his text.

The manuscript, like all Flecker's manuscripts, is a mass
of corrections. Almost every sentence has been emended –
his alterations were invariably improvements – and several
long episodes have been completely scrapped. These, however good, all went with excellent reason; the play would
be the worse were any of them restored. The scene in
Rafi's house has been very much reduced; both in large
and in little, Flecker's compressions, his squeezings out of
water from sentence and page, are admirable, briskness
being gained with every change. The first scene of the
next act has also been drastically cut, good but too rumina-
tive conversation between Hassan and the Caliph being
sacrificed. One example may be given of a passage as it was
(though this after many verbal alterations) and as it is.
Certain sentences ran thus:

CALIPH: Surely you are of gentle birth and do not know

your true origin. For how should a confectioner acquire the art of verse? Wherefore should a confectioner decorate his wall with a Bokhara carpet? In gems and miniatures and broidered silks I tested you at the Palace and you were surely a connoisseur. But never have I seen a man like you for poetry and carpets. When you tread on a carpet, you drop your eyes to earth to catch the pattern; and when you hear a poem, you raise your eyes to the stars to hear the tune.

HASSAN: No mystery, Master, attended thy servant's birth. My father was a confectioner, and his father too. If thou doubtest, look at me. Also have I the stature, the grace, the outline of nobility?

CALIPH: But whence your Poetry – and whence your carpets? Have you had a great teacher?

HASSAN: Master, I have not sat at the feet of the wise nor sucked honey from the lips of philosophers. But as for Poetry, I have learnt to read and I have loved to hear.

In the final version for print all this was brought down to:

CALIPH: What a man you are for poetry and carpets! When you tread on a carpet, you drop your eyes to earth and catch the pattern; and when you hear a poem, you raise your eyes to heaven to hear the tune. Whoever saw a confectioner like this! When did you learn poetry, Hassan of my heart?

HASSAN: In that great school, the Market of Bagdad ...

The scene in Hassan's pavilion was longer to the extent of an amusing episode. Hassan had his own Bokhara carpet brought to him from his house; its modest beauty did not blend with the gorgeousness of the Caliph's presents, but Hassan fought down objections with 'Roll up the Isfahani. What is harmony of colours to the presence of a friend?'

A long cut in the great Palace scene lopped a strand from the plot. As the play stands, Selim is never seen again after his disgraceful triumph over Hassan on Yasmin's balcony; we become well acquainted with him in the first Act and then he vanishes. Probably, in the original comedy, he remained an important character throughout; but only the opening scenes of the original comedy remain. There was no natural place for Selim in the later scenes of the play that ultimately grew out of the comedy; but Flecker did originally bring him in. He made him join the Beggars' rising and, in the Caliph's Hall, appeal to Hassan to obtain pardon for him. The Caliph gave Hassan the opportunity should he choose to take it; and Hassan, arguing with himself that it was unfair to the other doomed Beggars that one of their number should escape their fate, especially a rascal like Selim, refused to redeem him with the necessary word. Later on, this weighed on his conscience and the knowledge that he had sent an old friend to his doom made him wretched. The whole of this incident Flecker excised. He was probably aware that he had invented it merely in order to bring Selim in again and add another complication to the plot; he must certainly have realised that it weakened the appeal of Hassan to our sympathies and that he had loaded Hassan with enough tragedy without that; he may even have been doubtful whether the Hassan of his creation would have acted thus either from frigid logic or from long-cherished anger. At all events many pages of effective writing were struck out at a blow and the play greatly clarified and strengthened as a result. One more convolution of the plot was struck out. There was a passage in which the Caliph, at the last moment before the torture and death of Rafi and Pervaneh, told Hassan that if he really was so agonised by their sufferings, he could reprieve them by volunteering to take their place, thereby securing an immortality in poetry. Flecker wisely cut this out, knowing that it must impair the terrible grandeur of his direct conclusion, and that the rejection by Hassan of so intolerable an alternative would throw no new light whatever on his character, whilst diminishing, unfairly as it were, its attractiveness.

The play waited eight years for publication, at the request of those who had arranged to produce it on the stage. The long-delayed production is imminent as I write and those many who recently, after seeing the printed book, and those few who long ago, after reading the play in MS., were immediately convinced that Flecker had written a masterpiece, and a poet's masterpiece, are anxiously awaiting the test of the theatre. Flecker himself (writing to Mr Frank Savery) said: 'The part of the play that thrills me most is the ghosts – and don't you think the effect of the poem at the end should be grand? I love my ghosts – I suppose because my poetic soul loves the picturesque in the play above everything.' That is how he saw it when standing outside it and visualizing it as a theatrical construction: and certainly in *Hassan* are to be found some of the loveliest and most terrible spectacles which an English poet has ever imagined for the stage. But if, thinking of his achievement of beauty for the senses, of that realisation in colour and sound which he was never to see and hear, he talked of the grandeur of such effects, he knew well enough that into the tragic issue of his play he had poured 'exultations, agonies', passionate love and aspiration, torments which he was brave enough to face even if he could not master them: that he had registered here a struggle with the inexorable, and such dreams of the spirit as ring in Pervaneh's cry after her appalling and magnificent choice: 'Hark! Hark! — down through the spheres — the Trumpeter of Immortality! "Die lest I be shamed, lovers. Die, lest I be shamed." '

J. C. SQUIRE

ACT I

SCENE I

A room 'behind the shop' in old Bagdad. In the background a large caldron steaming, for the shop is a sweet-stuff shop and the sugar is boiling. The room has little furniture beyond a carpet, old but unexpectedly choice, and some Persian hangings (geometrical designs, with crude animals and some verses from the Koran hand-painted on linen). A ramshackle wooden partition in one corner shuts off from the living-room what appears to be the shop.

Squatting on the carpet — facing each other:

HASSAN, *the Confectioner, 45, rotund, moustache, turban, greasy grey dress.*

SELIM, *his friend, young, vulgarly handsome, gaudily clothed.*

HASSAN (*rocking on his mat*): Eywallah, Eywallah!

SELIM: Thirty-seven times have you made the same remark, O father of repetition.

HASSAN (*more dolefully than ever*): Eywallah, Eywallah!

SELIM: Have you caught fever? Is your chest narrow, or your belly thunderous?

HASSAN (*with a ponderous sigh*): Eywallah!

SELIM: Is that the merchant of sweetmeats, that sour face? O poisoner of children, surely it would be better to cut the knot of reluctance and uncord the casket of explanation. And the Poet Antari has justly remarked:

Divide your sorrow and impart your grief, O fool.
That good man comforteth beyond belief, O fool.

HASSAN (*inclining towards the mat*): None is good, save God. And Abou Awas has excellently sung:

The importunate
Are seldom fortunate.

Nevertheless, know, Selim, that I am in love.

SELIM: In love! Then why sit moaning on the mat? Are there not beauties at the barbers, and lights of love at the bazaar?

HASSAN (*angrily*): Hold your tongue, Selim, or leave me. I was in earnest when I said I loved, and your coarseness is ill-fitting to my mood. And well I know I am Hassan, the Confectioner, yet I can love as sincerely as Mejnun; for assuredly she on whom my heart is bent is not less fair than Leila.

SELIM (*ironically*): Alas! I mistook the particular for the general, and did not recognise the purity of your intentions. But I would not mention Mejnun. Mejnun was young, and you are old, and he was a prince, and you are a confectioner, and he was beautiful, and you are not, and he was very thin because of his sorrow, and you are fatter than those four-legged I mention not – God curse their herdsmen!

HASSAN: And if it be as you say, Selim, if I am indeed a fat, old, ugly tradesman, have I not good reason to be sorry and rock upon my mat, for how shall I attain my heart's desire?

SELIM: Listen to me, Hassan, why is it that in this last year you have become different from the Hassan that was Hassan? From time to time you talk strangely in your cups, like a mad poet; and you have bought a lute and a carpet too fine for your house. And now I fear you are losing your senses when I hear this talk of love from one who is past the age of folly.

HASSAN: It may be so, young man. Indeed, I think I am a fool. It is the affliction of Allah.

SELIM: Tell me, at least, who she is. It may be she is not so unattainable as you imagine, unless indeed you have set eyes on the Caliph's daughter, or on the Queen of all the Jinn.

HASSAN: Listen, Selim, and I will tell you my affair. Three days ago a woman came here to buy loukoum of me, dressed as a widow, and bade me follow her to her door with the parcel. Alas, Selim! I could see her eyes beneath the veil, and they were like the twin fountains in the Caliph's garden; and her lips beneath her veil were like roses hidden in moss, and her waist was flexible as a palm-tree swaying in the wind, and her hips were large and heavy and round, like water melons in the season of water melons. And I glanced at her but she would not smile, and I sighed but she would not glance, and the door of her house shut fast against me, like the gate of Paradise against an infidel. Eywallah!

(Recommences moaning.)

SELIM: And where was the house of this widow who bought sweetmeats and had none to sell?

HASSAN: In the street of Felicity, by the fountain of the Two Pigeons.

SELIM (*musing*): It must be the widow of that Achmet they hung last year by the Basra Gate.

HASSAN: Which Achmet?

SELIM: The hairy one.

HASSAN: Istagfurallah! He fluttered like a bird. May I never soar so high.

SELIM: Istagfurallah! May I see you! I should burst with laughter and the vultures with repletion. But tell me, you who have fallen so deep in love, do you rejoice in your misfortune like a dervish in his dirt, or do you honestly desire satisfaction?

HASSAN: I desire satisfaction, Selim. But I pray you, talk no more of this.

SELIM: Well, take courage, faint heart, since all things can be cured save perversity in asses. Perhaps I can cure you of love.

HASSAN: By the Prophet, Selim, do not cure my love, cure her indifference.

SELIM (*with sudden alertness*): There is only one way of doing that.

HASSAN: Which way?

SELIM: Do you believe in magic, Hassan?

HASSAN: Men who think themselves wise believe nothing till the proof. Men who are wise believe anything till the disproof.

SELIM: What do we know if magic be a lie or not? But, since it is certain that only magic can avail you, you may as well put it to the test. You can buy a philtre that can draw her love, and send her a jar of magic sweets.

HASSAN: I am ready to all things, ingenious Selim; but do you know a good magician?

SELIM: Zachariah, the Jew, has but lately arrived from Aleppo: he is the talk of all the market-place, and a wonderful man if tales be true.

HASSAN: Have you the tales?

SELIM: I have this among many. They say that in Bokhara a man called him an offensive Jew and flung a stone at his head: and he caused the stone to be suspended in the air and the man too, so that the man walked all round Bokhara over the heads of the passersby, who were astonished, and was constrained to enter his house by the upper window.

HASSAN (*incredulous*): Mashallah!

SELIM: And stranger than that. At Ispahan men say he took off the dome of the Great Mosque and turned it round and had a bath in it, and put it back again.

HASSAN: Mashallah!

SELIM: And strangest of all, at Cairo, for the amusement of the Sultan, he turned the whole population into apes for half an hour.

HASSAN: A very trifling change if we knew the Egyptians. I don't believe a word of all these tales. Yet, doubtless he is a good enough physician to make a love philtre. But are philtres any good?

SELIM: There can be no doubt that there are philtres which drive women to love, though their hearts be as strong and their heads as cold as the mountains of Qaf. But as for this Zachariah, I know he sells philtres at ten dinars the bottle: his shop is crowded with rich old women.

HASSAN: Eywallah, Selim, I am sick of love; no damsel is worth ten dinars. And sages have remarked, 'The ideal is expensive!' and philosophers have observed, 'There are a thousand figs on the fig-tree and all as like as like.'

SELIM: What! All the smooth, shining hills and well-wooded valleys in that country of love ... all going for ten dinars! ... And this is the man whose love is like Mejnun's! What is ten dinars to a man in love? You gave thrice that sum for this carpet.

HASSAN: A carpet is a carpet, and a woman is a woman.

23

It is not only the ten dinars. But you know that in this market I have a character. 'Hassan', men say, 'is a safe man. Hassan will not leave his jacket on the wall, or buy peas without prodding the sack'. But if they hear: 'A stranger came to Bagdad and no Mussulman and said he would do this, and Hassan has paid him ten dinars and got no gain', they will nudge each other when I walk abroad at evening, and say: 'A sad end'; and another, 'Look at him, Saadet, my son, and drink no wine'; and another, 'God preserve me from the friends of such a one!' And they will call out to me as they pass, 'Ya Hassan, give me ten dinars that I may build a mosque!' And I shall be shamed where I was honoured, and abased where I was exalted ...

(*A loud knocking on the floor of the adjacent shop causes* HASSAN *to retire thither hurriedly. As he disappears* YAS-MIN *peeps inquisitively, unveiled, through the little window in the partition.*)

SELIM: What an impudent little beauty ... Why, she had a widow's scarf on. She must be the princess! (*Rocks with laughter.*) The unattainable ideal! And I have her address. It requires a frenzied lover to pay cash for a flask of coloured water. But I doubt if Hassan's sweets mingled with coloured water will do aught but make her sick. Whereas a cake stuffed with those very dinars ... Allah, the dinars would not choke her! O thou fool Hassan!

> *Tell not thy shirt who smiled and answered 'Yes':*
> *Dream not her name, nor fancy her address.*

(*Enter* HASSAN, *pale and staggering.*)

HASSAN: Selim, in the name of friendship, take these ten dinars and buy me that philtre, and return with speed.

SELIM (*feigning irritation*): Allah! Am I your messenger? Go yourself to the Jew.

HASSAN: I must prepare the sweetmeats this very hour, to send them to her before sunset. In the name of friendship, Selim, take the dinars and purchase me the philtre.

SELIM (*rising and taking dinars*): Do not make me chargeable, O Hassan, if the philtre is without effect. I only repeat what I have heard.

HASSAN: No, I will not blame you. But go quickly for the magic that nothing may be left unsampled that may prove beneficial.

(*Exit* SELIM; HASSAN *makes up the fire and prepares his caldron, saying meanwhile*)

That young man weareth out my carpet apace. I begin to think also he doth fray the braid of my affection. But if he buys me a good philtre I will forgive him. Oh, cruel destiny, thou hast made me a common man with a common trade. My friends are fellows from the market, and all my worthless family is dead. Had I been rich, ah me! how deep had been my delight in matters of the soul, in poetry and music and pictures, and companions who do not jeer and grin, and above all, in the colours of rich carpets and expensive silks. But be content, O artist: thou hast one carpet; be content, confectioner: thou hast one love – one love, but unattained ... yet hadst thou been rich, O confectioner, never hadst thou found her.

Now I will make her sweets, such sweets, ah me! as never I made in my life before. I will make her sweets like globes of crystal, like cubes of jade, like polygons of ruby. I will make her sweets like flowers. Great red roses, passionate carnations, raying daisies, violets, and curly hyacinths. I will perfume my roses (may they

25

melt sweetly in her lips) with the perfume of roses, so that she shall say 'a rose'! and smell before she tastes. And in the heart of each flower I will distil one drop of the magic of love. Did I not say 'they shall be flowers'?

SCENE II

Moonlight. The Street of Felicity by the Fountain of the Two Pigeons. A house with a balcony on either side of the street. In front of one of the houses, HASSAN, *cloaked: a* PORTER.

HASSAN: Has she received the box, O guardian of the door of separation?

PORTER: From my hands, O dispenser of bounty.

HASSAN: What did thy mistress say?

PORTER: Sir, the hands of mediation are empty.

HASSAN (*giving a dinar*): I have filled them. What honey dropped from that golden mouth?

PORTER: She said – may thy servant find grace – 'Curses on the fat sugar cook and his love-sick eyes. Allah be praised, his confectionery is better than his countenance!'

HASSAN (*aside*): If she likes the confectionery, all may be well. And what didst thou reply?

PORTER: I said: 'His sweets sparkle like diamonds and rubies in the crown of our Caliph, and his sugar is as pure as his intentions.' And she answered – the protection on thy slave – 'His intentions may be pure, but his coat is greasy.'

HASSAN: And did she eat the confectionery?

PORTER: I do not know. But within the hour I removed the box, and it was empty.

HASSAN: Ah! Salaam and thanks.

PORTER: And to thee the Salaam.

HASSAN: But tell me what is the name of thy mistress?

PORTER: Yasmin is her name, Sir.

HASSAN: A sweet name for a moonlight night. Salaam aleikum.

PORTER: Ya Hawaja, v'aleikum assalam!

(*The* PORTER *returns and shuts the gate.*)

HASSAN (*to himself*): What if the Jews are an older race than we and know old forgotten secrets? Alas, I believe no more in these Israelitish sweets. Could those drops of purple liquid command the spirit of love? And yet, who can say? The young men of the market-place laugh at all enchantments – but do they know how to spin the sun? On a night like this, does not the very fountain sing in tune and enchant the dropping stones? Ah, Yasmin? (*Taking out lute from beneath his cloak and tuning it.*) Yasmin ... Yasmin ... Yasmin ... Yasmin.

(*Intones to the accompaniment of the lute.*)

How splendid in the morning glows the lily; with what grace he throws

His supplication to the rose: do roses nod the head, Yasmin?

But when the silver dove descends I find the little flower of friends,

Whose very name that sweetly ends, I say when I have said, Yasmin.

The morning light is clear and cold; I dare not in that light behold

A whiter light, a deeper gold, a glory too far shed, Yasmin.

But when the deep red eye of day is level with the lone highway,

And some to Mecca turn to pray, and I toward thy bed, Yasmin,

27

Or when the wind beneath the moon is drifting like a
soul aswoon,

And harping planets talk love's tune with milky wings
outspread, Yasmin,

Shower down thy love, O burning bright! for one night
or the other night

Will come the Gardener in white, and gathered flowers
are dead, Yasmin!

(*As* HASSAN *intones the last 'Yasmin' with passion the shutters open, and* YASMIN, *veiled, looks out.*)

YASMIN: Alas, Minstrel, Yasmin is my name also, but it
was for a fairer Yasmin than me, I fear, you have strung
these pearls.

HASSAN: There is no Yasmin but Yasmin, and you are
Yasmin.

YASMIN: Can this be Hassan, the Confectioner?

HASSAN: I am Hassan, and I am a confectioner.

YASMIN: Mashallah, Hassan, your words are sweeter than
your sweets.

HASSAN: Gracious lady, your eyes look down through
your veil like angels through a cloud. Dare I ask to see
your face, O bright perfection?

YASMIN (*roguishly*): Do you take me for a Christian,
father of impertinence? And since when do the daughters of Islam unveil before strangers?

HASSAN: It is said: he who speaks to the heart is no
stranger.

YASMIN (*unveiling her eyes*): Are you satisfied, O importunate!

HASSAN: Never, till I have seen perfection to perfection.

YASMIN: You would shrivel, my poet. What about 'the
glory too far shed, Yasmin'?

HASSAN: Let me see you unveiled, Yasmin.

YASMIN: Anything to close the portal of your face. (*Unveiling.*) There. Do I please thee, my Sultan?

HASSAN (*rapturously*): Oh, you are beautiful!

YASMIN: Prince of poets, is that all you have to say! Not a stanza, not a trope, not a turn, not a twist, not even a hint that the heavens are opened, or that there are two moons in the sky together?

HASSAN: There is but one.

YASMIN: Well confectioned, my confectioner! And now, Good-night.

HASSAN: O stay, Yasmin, you are too beautiful and I too bold. I am nothing, and you are the Queen of the Stars of Night. But the thought of you is twisted in the strings of my heart; I burn with love of you, Yasmin. Put me to the proof, my lady; there is nothing I could not do for your bright eyes. I would cross the salt desert and wrest the cup of the water of life from the Jinn that guards it; I would walk to the barriers of the world and steal the roc's egg from its diamond nest. I would swim the seven oceans, and cross the five islands to rob Solomon ben Dawud of his ring in the palace where he lies sleeping in the silence and majesty of un-corrupting death. And I would slip the ring on your finger and make you mistress of the spirits of the air — but would you love me? Could you love me, do you love me, Yasmin?

YASMIN: There is love and love and love.

HASSAN (*passionately*): Oh, answer me!

YASMIN: I think I have been enchanted, Hassan; how, I cannot tell. Till this afternoon the thought of your appearance made my heart narrow with disgust. But since I ate your present of comfits — and they were admirable comfits, and I ate them with speed — my heart is changed and inclined toward you, I know not why or how, except it be through magic.

HASSAN (*aside*): She is mine, and magic rules the world! (*Aloud*): Yasmin, shall I possess you, O Yasmin?

YASMIN: Am I not a desert waiting for the rain? Was I not born for passion, Hassan? Is not my bosom burning for kisses? Were not these arms made smooth and hard to fight the battle of love?

HASSAN: Are not your lips love's roses, your cheeks love's lilies, your eyes love's hyacinths?

YASMIN: Ya, Hassan, and my hair the net of love, and my girdle the chain of love that breaks at a lover's touch?

HASSAN: I am drowning in a wave of madness. Let me in, Yasmin; let me in!

YASMIN: Ah, if I could!

HASSAN: Why not?

YASMIN: Ah, if I dared!

HASSAN: What do you fear? It is night, and the street is silent.

YASMIN: Ah, dear Hassan, but I am not alone.

HASSAN (*whispering*): Not alone? Who is there? Your mother?

YASMIN: No! One whom you sent here.

HASSAN: I sent no one.

YASMIN: One of your friends.

HASSAN: A man?

SELIM (*poking his head out of the window*): Ya, Hassan, Salaam aleikum. I thank you for directing my steps to this rose-strewn bower.

HASSAN (*astonished*): Selim!

SELIM: Thy servant always.

HASSAN (*wildly*): Selim!

SELIM: Be advised, O Hassan, go and seek the enchanted egg.

HASSAN: Selim, what do you here?

SELIM: Plunge not the finger of enquiry into the pie of impertinence, O my uncle.

HASSAN: Since when have I become your uncle, Selim, and how did I cease to be your friend?

SELIM: Since when did you aspire to poetry, O Hassan? but I have heard these lines:

> *As from the eagle flies the dove*
> *So friendship from the claw of love.*

HASSAN: Love. What love do you mean, scum of the market?

SELIM: This. (*Puts a hand on* YASMIN'S *shoulder.*)

HASSAN: May God strike thee blind, Selim, and shut the door of his compassion against thee!

SELIM: What is my crime, Uncle? How have I sinned against thee, or merited this solemn imprecation?

HASSAN: Do not touch her, you dog, do not touch her!

SELIM: Is it a crime to touch Yasmin, my Uncle? Am I not to be excused? Is not her neck a pillar of the marble of Yoonistan? (*Puts his arm round her neck.*)

HASSAN: Torment of death!

YASMIN: Are not my arms like swords of steel, hard and cold, and thirsty for blood? (*Putting her arms round the neck of* SELIM.)

HASSAN: Fire of hell!

SELIM: Are not her eyes two sapphires in two pools?

HASSAN: Woe is me! Woe is me!

YASMIN: Are not my lips two rubies drenched in blood? (*Kisses him.*)

31

HASSAN: God, I shall fall!

SELIM (*his face in* YASMIN'S *bosom*: Couldst thou but see, O my Uncle, the silver hills with their pomegranate groves; or the deep fountain in the swelling plain, or the Ethiopian who waters the roses in the garden, or the great lamp between the columns where the incense of love is burned. How can I thank thee, O my Uncle, for the name and address, and half the old Jew's dinars!

YASMIN: How can I thank thee, O my Uncle, for sending me this strong and straight young friend of thine to console my loneliness and desolation? Ah, it is bitter to be a widow and so young!

HASSAN (*putting up his hands to his head*): The fountain, the fountain! O my head, my head!

YASMIN: Be not too rash, my Uncle, or thy hair will come away in thy hands.

HASSAN: If I could but reach your necks with a knife, children of Sheitan!

YASMIN: I was the sun of his existence, and now I am a child of Sheitan — and why? Never again will I trust the love of a man. I was a glory too far shed, and now he wants to open my neck. And already he has tried to poison me. Ya, Hassan, if you desire my death, send me some more enchanted sweets!

SELIM: Beware, O Hassan, of jesting with the Jinn.

YASMIN: Buy, O Hassan, no more juice from Jews.

SELIM: Much I fear, O my friend, for thy character in the market. No more will men say, 'Hassan is a safe man'; but they will nudge each other and say, 'Beware of Hassan, Hassan is a great magician; he has talked with the spirits of the air! Deal not with Hassan, O my son, Saadet, for he sells enchanted sweets that drive the consumer to madness. And at night Hassan becomes a cat, and walketh on the roofs after the female cats. Allah preserve me from the evil eye of such a one!' And another will say, tapping his forehead, 'Speak no harm of poor Hassan, for his brain is very sick!' And the small, guileless boys will say, 'Behold Hassan, who gave ten dinars for a pint of indigo and water!'

HASSAN: Ah, death!

YASMIN: Look at him! He is drifting like a soul aswoon! Go home, old fellow!

SELIM: Go home, and write poems!

YASMIN: Go home, and cook sweets!

HASSAN: Yasmin! Yasmin! My head!

YASMIN: Begone, or I will cool thy head, thou wearisome old fool!

HASSAN: Yasmin! Yasmin! (*Stands with his arms outstretched.*)

YASMIN: Take this, my bulbul, to quench thy aspiration. (*Pours a jug of water over him, and slams the shutters to. HASSAN does not budge from his position.*)

HASSAN: O thou villainous, unclean dog, Selim. O thou unutterable woman. I will have you both whipped through the city and impaled in the market-place, and your bodies flung to rot on a dung-heap. O, my head aches! Ah, you foul swine! May you scream in hell for ever. O, my head – my head. For ever. Thou and thy magic and thy Jew. There is blood dripping from the wall. (*Banging on the gate.*) I will break the house in. I will kill you. Ya Allah, I am splitting in twain. It is my own fault for having dreams and believing magic. Ya Allah, I am dying. Oh, Yasmin, so beautiful, so brutal. O burning bright; you have killed me! Farewell, and the Salaam!

(Falls under the shadow of the fountain. Silence. A light appears in the next house. Soft music starts; the first light of dawn shines in the sky.)

(Enter the CALIPH HAROUN AR RASCHID, JAFAR, *his Vizier,* MASRUR *(a Negro), his executioner, and* ISHAK, *a young man, his poet, all attired as Merchants.)*

CALIPH: Ishak, my heart is heavy, and still the night drags on, and still we wander in the crooked streets, and still we find no entertainment, and still the white moon shines.

ISHAK: O Caliph of Islam, is there not vast entertainment for the wise in the shining of the moon, in the dripping of that fountain, and in the shape of that tall cypress that has leapt the wall to shoot her arrow at the stars?

(The music which had stopped recommences.)

CALIPH: But I hear music, and see lights. Come on, come on, we will snatch profit from this cursed night even yet, my friends, even at the eleventh hour.

JAFAR: Master, the night is far advanced, and you have not slept. It is a late hour to seek for entertainment.

CALIPH: Jafar, you are as prudent as a shopkeeper.

ISHAK: There lies his merit, Haroun! For he keeps the great shop of state, he sells the revenue of provinces, and buys in the lives of men.

CALIPH: Enough, enough. Call to them, Jafar, and see if they will let us in.

JAFAR: Oh, gentlefolk, in the name of Allah!

VOICE *(from window, the person invisible)*: Who calls?

JAFAR: Sir, we are four merchants who came yesterday night from Basra, and on our arrival we met in the street a man of Basra settled in Bagdad, who prayed us to dine with him. So we accepted and stayed late talking the talk of Basra, and left him but an hour ago. And

34

since we were strangers to the city, we lost our way, and have been wandering ever since in search of our Khan and have not found it. And now a happy chance has taken us to this street; for seeing lights and hearing music, indeed, sir, we hope to taste the cup of they kindness, being men of honour, good companions and true believers.

VOICE: Then you are not of Bagdad?

JAFAR: No, sir, but of Basra.

VOICE: Had you been of Bagdad, you should not have entered for all the gold in the Caliph's coffers.

CALIPH: Then we may enter, being of Basra?

VOICE: If you enter, you will be in my power. And if you annoy me, I will punish you with death. But no one constraineth you to enter. Go in peace, O men of Basra.

CALIPH (*aside*): A rare adventure. (*Aloud.*) We take the risk of annoying you, O host of terror, and are now looking for the door.

VOICE: Since when did a door of good reputation open on to this street, my masters? Our door is far from here, and you are strangers and merry, and will not find it. But I will contrive a means for your ascent.

CALIPH: Jafar, I never suspected there was a great house in this poor quarter of the town. For from the outside it is a house like any other, except that it has no door; but inside, if this is but the back of it, it is of great extent and holds some secret. We shall make a discovery to-night, O Jafar.

JAFAR: Master, we have been warned of danger!

(*A basket comes down.*)

CALIPH: Danger? What care I?

(*Sits in the basket, and is drawn up.*)

JAFAR: Eh, Masrur, I could sleep a little.

35

MASRUR: You would wake in Paradise if the Caliph heard you, Jafar.

(MASRUR *waves his sword dexterously near* JAFAR'S *neck*.)

JAFAR (*as he ascends into the basket, pointing to* MASRUR'S *sword*): The path to Paradise is narrow and shiny, O Masrur!

MASRUR (*with a grim motion of the sword*): Ya, Jafar, it is a short cut.

(JAFAR *having ascended,* MASRUR *ascends, and the basket is let down for* ISHAK.)

ISHAK (*alone*): Go on thy way without me, Commander of the Faithful. I will follow you no further. Find one more adventure if you will. For me the break of day is adventure enough – and the water splashing in the fountain. Find out, Haroun, the secret of the lights and of the music, of the house that has no door, and the master that will admit no citizen. Drag out the mystery of a man's love or loss, then break your oath and publish his tale to all Bagdad, then fling him gold, and fling him gold, and dream you have made a friend! Those bags of gold you fling, O my generous master, to a mistress for a night, to a poet for a jest, to a rich friend for an entertainment, to a beggar for a whim, are they not the revenues of cities, wrung by torture from the poor? But the sighs of your people, Haroun, do not so much as stir the leaves in your palace garden!

And I – I have taken your gold, I, Ishak, who was born on the mountains free of the woods and winds. I have made my home in your palaces, and almost forgot it was a prison. And for you I have strung glittering, fulsome verses, a hundred rhyming to one rhyme, ingeniously woven, my disgrace as a poet, my dishonour as a man. And I have forgotten that there are men who

36

dig and sow, and a hut on the hills where I was born. (*Perceives* HASSAN.) Ah, there is a body, here in the shade. The corpses of the poor are very common in the streets these days. They die of poison or the knife, but most of hunger. Mashallah, but you have not died of hunger, my friend, and there is that on your face I do not like to see. By his clothes this was a common man, a grocer or a baker, his person ill-proportioned and unseemly, but by his forehead not quite a common man. I think –

JAFAR (*from above*): Ishak, are you coming up?

ISHAK (*shouting back*): Wait a minute, I will come.

(*To himself.*) What has curved his mouth into that bitter line? He is an ugly man, but I maintain there is grace in his countenance.

What? a lute? Take my hand, O brother. You loved music too, and you could sing the songs of the people, which are better than mine – the songs I learnt from the mother of my mother. (*Taking the broken lute mechanically.*) What was that one?

> '*The Green Boy came from over the mountains,*
> *Joy of the morning, joy of his heart*'?

I have forgotten it, and the lute is broken. Or that other:

> '*Come to the wells, the desert wells!*
> *The caravan is marching down; I hear the camel bells.*'

(*Resumes* HASSAN's *hand.*) Ah, brother, your hand is warm and your heart beating, you are not dead. (*Bathing* HASSAN's *forehead with water from the fountain.*) I shall know after all what has twisted your mouth awry.

CALIPH: Ishak, Ishak, we wait and wait.

37

ISHAK: May I not be free one hour, to breathe the dawn alone! Ah! ... (*Takes* HASSAN's *body and drags it to the basket.*) I come, my master! (*Puts* HASSAN *in the basket.*) There, take my place, brother, and find your destiny. I will be free to-night, free for one dawn upon the hills! (*As* HASSAN *is drawn up in the basket,* ISHAK *walks rapidly away.*)

CURTAIN

ACT II

A great room. To the left three arches lead out on to a balcony where the personages CALIPH, JAFAR *and* HOST *are collected. The interior of the room is blazing with lights, but empty. The architecture of the room is curious on account of the wide, low arches which cut off a square in the centre. The furniture of the room is in rich, rather vulgar Oriental taste.*

CALIPH: Ishak, Ishak, we are waiting and waiting.

JAFAR: Ishak! Ishak! Perhaps he is faint.

CALIPH: Faint!

JAFAR: Let me go down and see what he is doing. I think I hear him talking.

CALIPH: He is talking to shadows. He has one of his evil fits to-night. Do not trouble your head or mine about him. He presumes on our friendship, and forgets the respect due to us. Am I to be kept waiting like a Jew in a court of justice, I the Master ...

JAFA (*quickly*): We are not in Basra, Sir. But see, the rope has tightened. (*To* MASRUR.) Haul, thou whose soul is white.

RAFI (*Host*) (*helping with ropes to* CALIPH *who stands idle*): God restore to you the use of your arms, my brother from Basra.

(HASSAN *rolls out of the basket, filthy and inanimate.*)
Yallah, Yallah, on what dunghill did this fowl die? Is this your man of honour?

39

JAFAR (*astonished*): Host of the house, this is not our companion, and we have never set eyes on him before.

RAFI: Then what is this?

CALIPH: Our friend has played a trick on us – may Allah separate him from salvation! – and sent up this body in place of himself. Come, let us tip it out into the street.

RAFI (*feeling* HASSAN'S *pulse*): Wait; this man is by no means dead, and the mill of his heart still grinds the flour of life. Ho, Alder!

(*Enter* ALDER, *a young and pretty page.*)

ALDER: At his master's service.

RAFI: Ho, Willow!

WILLOW (*younger still*): At his lord's order.

RAFI: Juniper!

JUNIPER: At his Pasha's command.

RAFI: Tamarisk!

TAMARISK (*a little boy with a squeaky voice*): At his Sublimity's feet.

CALIPH (*aside to* JAFAR): Truly, this is charming: an illustrious example of decorum and good taste.

RAFI: Transform this into a man, my slaves. Revive him, bathe, soap, scent, comb him, clothe him with a ceremonial coat and bring him back to us.

ALDER: We hear,

WILLOW: We honour,

JUNIPER: We tremble,

TAMARISK: and obey.

CALIPH (*entering the great room of the house*): Thy house is of grand proportions and eccentric architecture, my Host; it is astonishing that such a house should look out on to so mean a street.

RAFI: It is an old house wherein the Manichees (the devil roast all heretics!) once held their meetings before they

40

were all flayed alive. It is called the house of the moving
walls.

CALIPH: Why such a name?

RAFI: I do not know at all.

CALIPH: The merry noise of music that we heard is silent.

RAFI: I waited for your permission, my guests, before
continuing my meagre entertainment. Ho, music! Ho,
dancers! (*Claps his hands.*)

(*Music plays. The* HOST *enters the room and motions his*
GUESTS *to be seated in silence.*)

CALIPH: Verily, after this prelude, and in this splendid
palace, we shall see dancing women worthy of Paradise.

JAFAR: God grant it, Master.

CALIPH (*to* JAFAR): Hush, I hear the pattering of feet.
The wine of anticipation is dancing through my veins.
O Jafar, what incomparable houris will charm our eyes
to-night? What rosy breasts, what silver shoulders,
what shapely legs, what jasmine arms!

(*In good order, marching to the music, there enter the most
awful selection of Eastern* BEGGARS *the eye could imagine,
or the tongue describe. They are headed by their* CHIEF, *a
rather fine fellow, in indescribable tatters. He leads the*
CHORUS *with a song, half intoned in the Oriental style.*)

> Fathers of two feet, advance,
>   Dot and go ones, hop along,
> Two feet missing need not dance,
>   But will join us in the song.

CHORUS OF CULS-DE-JATTE:

> But will join you in the song.

> Show your most revolting scar;
>   People never weary of it.

41

The more nauseous you are –
    More their pity and your profit.

CHORUS:
    And your profit, profit, profit.

Cracked of lip and gapped of tooth,
    Apoplectic, maim or mad,
Blind of one eye, blind of both,
    Up, the beggars of Bagdad.

CHORUS:
    Up, the beggars of Bagdad.

There's a cellar, I am told,
    Where a little lamp is lit,
And that cellar's full of gold,
    Sacks and sacks and sacks of it.

CHORUS (*hoarsely*):
    Sacks and sacks and sacks of it,
    Stacks and stacks and stacks of it.
    Open eyes and stiffen backs,
    There are sacks and sacks and sacks;
    And gold for him who lacks of it.

(*The* HOST *lifts his hand. The* BEGGARS *all fall flat on their faces. Dance music.*)
(*Enter right, a* BAND *of fair, left, a* BAND *of dusky beauties.*)

THE DANCING GIRLS:
    Daughters of delight, advance,
      Petals, petals, drift along;
    Cypress, tremble! Firefly, dance!
      Nightingale, your song, your song!

THE FAIR: We are pale
THE DARK: as dawn, with roses,
    O the roses, O desire!
    We are dark,

THE FAIR (*curtsying*):
>> but as the twilight
> Shooting all the sky with fire.

CHORUS:
>> Daughters of delight, advance.
>> Petals, petals, drift along,
>> Cypress, tremble! Firefly, dance!
>> Nightingale, your song, your song!

(*They surround the* BEGGARS, *dancing, and point at them.*)

LEADER OF THE FAIR:
> From what base tavern, of what street
> Were dragged these dogs, that foul our feet?

LEADER OF THE DARK:
> O sisters, fly, we shall be hurt:

> (*The* LEADER OF THE BEGGARS *catches her.*)
> Leave go my ankle, son of dirt.

LEADER OF THE BEGGARS:
> Lady, if the dirt should gleam,
>> Feel, but do not show surprise:
> Things that happen here would seem

(*Rises to his feet, his rags drop off, and he shines in gold.*)
>> Paradox in Paradise.

(*The infirmities and rags of the whole* BAND *disappear as if by magic, as they rise and shout in* CHORUS.)

CHORUS:
>> Paradox in Paradise.

(RAFI *raises his hand.* ALL *stand at attention.*)

VOICES:
>> Hush, the King speaks.
>> The King of the Beggars.
>> The King.

LEADER OF THE BEGGARS: The King of the Beggars,

the Caliph of the Faithless, the Peacock of the Silver Path, the Master of Bagdad!

(*The* BALLET *line the room behind the arches.*)

JAFAR (*aside, astonished*): King of the Beggars?

MASRUR (*aside, astonished*): Master of Bagdad?

CALIPH (*aside, astonished*): Caliph of the Faithless? Allah kerim, this is a jest indeed!

RAFI (*throwing off his outer garment and discovering himself superbly dressed in a golden armour*): Subjects and Guests. Now that the night before our day is ending, and the Wolf's Tail is already brushing the eastern sky; now that our plot is ready, our conspiracy established, our victory imminent, what is there left for me to tell you, O faithful band? Shall I say, be brave? You are lions. Be cunning? You are serpents. Be bloody? You are wolves.

See now, Bagdad is still in dreams that in a few minutes shall be full of fire, and that fire redder than the dawn. You have begged – you shall buy: you have fawned – you shall fight: you have plotted – you shall plunder: you have cringed: you shall kill.

How loud they snore, those swine whose nostrils we shall slit to-day! Copper they flung to us, and steel we shall give them back; good steel of Damascus, that digs a narrow hole and deep.

But as for the Peacock of Peacocks, that sack of debauch, that Caliph, alive in his coffin, I and none other will nail him down, with his eyes staring into mine. His gardens, fountains, summer-houses, and palaces; his horses, mules, camels, and elephants, his statues of Yoonistan, and his wines of Ferangistan, his eunuchs of Egypt, and his carpets of Bokhara, and his great sealed boxes bursting with unbeaten gold, and his beads of

44

amethyst, and his bracelets of sapphire, all this and all his women, his chosen flower-like women, are yours for lust and loot and lechery, my children – all save her of whom I warned you – the woman who is mine, and who shall sit unveiled with me on the throne of all the Caliphs ... and when you see us sitting on that throne together, then you shall cry ...

THE BEGGARS (*taking up with a shout*): The Caliph is dead! The Caliphate is over! Long live the King!

JAFAR (*in indignation*): These words are not holy, even in jest.

RAFI: O guests of an hour, I pray you put the tongue of discretion into the cheek of propriety.

JAFAR: Propriety! The host's obligations are greater than the guests. It is not good taste to speak thus before the invited. We pray you only that we may withdraw at once.

RAFI: And who will withdraw me, my masters, from the vengeance of the Caliph, once you have talked a talk with the Captain of his Guard?

JAFAR: We give you our promise: we are men of honour.

RAFI: If you were thieves, as we are, I might trust you. But, if, as you say, you are men of honour, honour will drive you panting to the Caliph's gate, and honour will swiftly break a promise made to a thief and a rebel, under compulsion.

JAFAR: Sir, I pray you, no more of this, be it jest or earnest. It will soon be morning: we must away: we have pressing business: our clients await us.

RAFI: Give me their names, O my guests, and to-night I will fling their gold and their carcases together at your feet.

JAFAR: We insist that you let us go.

RAFI: O merchants, tell me but this one thing: do you dwell in fine houses in the port of Basra?

JAFAR: We have no mean abodes.

RAFI: Are your apartments spacious and well furnished?

JAFAR: Well enough.

RAFI: And tell me further, have you soft carpets on the floors of those rooms?

JAFAR: There are carpets.

RAFI: Great, rich, soft carpets from Persia and Afghanistan?

JAFAR: Yes.

RAFI: It is a pity. Soft carpets make soft the sole of the foot. And they who have soft feet should ever keep them in the road of meekness.

MASRUR (*drawing his sword*): Dost thou dare threaten us, bismillah!

RAFI: Truly, O most disgusting negro, comprehension and thou have been separated since your youth. Shall I then drop the needle of insinuation and pick up the club of statement? Shall I tell you three guests of mine, with the plainness of plainness and the openness of plainness, that if you offer one threat more, propose one evasion more, or ask one question more, I will thrash your lives head downwards from your feet.

(*Enter* HASSAN *finely dressed, ushered in by the* FOUR BOYS *through the rows of* DANCERS.)

HASSAN (*lamenting*): Eywallah, eywallah, eywah, eywah, Mashallah! Istagfurallah!

RAFI: Why, here is the fourth guest!

ALDER: We have washed him: he needed it.

WILLOW: Combed him: it was necessary.

JUNIPER: Scented him: it was our duty.

TAMARISK: Clothed him: it was our delight.

46

HASSAN (*as before*): Eywallah! Yallah Akbar! Y'allah kerim! Istagfurallah! Eywallah! Hassan is ended! Hassan is no more! He is dead! He is buried! He is a bone! Y'allah kerim!

RAFI: Eyyah Hassan, if that is your name, have my boys not treated you well? If they have hurt you with their tricks, by the Great Name, I will ...

HASSAN: I pray you, I pray you. Thrash no one's life out downwards from their feet, O master, and above all, not mine.

RAFI: Ah, you heard me! Take courage. All that I require of my guests, good Hassan, is genteel behaviour.

HASSAN: Ah! Who are these terrible men?

RAFI: Beggars of Bagdad! Ten thousand more await my signal in the streets. In a few minutes they will surprise the drowsy Palace Guards, sack Bagdad, kill the Caliph and make me King.

HASSAN (*stupefied*): What has become of me this night! Just now I was in Hell, with all the fountains raining fire and blood.

RAFI: Come, Hassan, you are only just in time; the cold dawn which ends the revellers' dark day will soon be uncurtaining the blue. One bowl to pledge me victory, O guests, for I must away and win it, and you shall lie here to sleep away the destruction of Bagdad. At least you shall say this of your host – he gave us splendid wine.

(*The* FOUR SLAVES *hand round the bowl; the* CALIPH *refuses.*)

(*To* CALIPH): Sir, you do not drink.

CALIPH: I obey the Prophet.

RAFI: What wine do they grow in the desert of Meccah, or on the sandhills of Medina? Ah, had the Prophet tasted wine of Syria or the islands, the book would have been shorter by that uncomfortable verse.

JAFAR: Come, host! I at all events will pledge you. There is ever fellowship between those who have drunk wine together, be they murderers or thieves or Christians.

MASRUR: Host, on the day when I shall spill your blood, I shall drink a little in remembrance of this bowl of wine. Till then your health! (*Drinks.*)

RAFI (*sarcastically*): Ye are three jolly fellows of amiable dispositions. (*Drinks.*) I thank you, negro, I drink to yours.

HASSAN: I drink to forget a woman, but will this little cup suffice?

RAFI: Nor ten, nor ten thousand little cups like these, if you have loved. To-night I shall fill my bowl of oblivion with the blood of the Caliph of Bagdad. Brother, will that great cup suffice?

HASSAN (*in terror*): Call me not brother, thou savage man, who dost dare talk of shedding the holiest blood in Islam!

RAFI: When high office is polluted, when the holy is unholy, when justice is a lie, when the people are starved, and the great fools of the world in high office, then dares a man talk of shedding the holiest blood in Islam.

CALIPH: Also when one has a vengeance to wreak on the Caliph and a claim on a lady of his household.

MASRUR: Why do you want to nail him in his coffin alive? Tell us the tale.

JAFAR: Tell us, if you would not have us think you a madman or a buffoon.

CALIPH: Tell us about the woman; what harm can it do you since we are in your power?

Rafi (*after hesitation*): Yes, what harm can it do, if for my own sake, to relieve the heaviness of my heart, I tell you something of my story?

My name is Rafi. I come from the hills beyond Mosul, where the men walk free and the women go unveiled. There I was betrothed to Pervaneh, a woman beautiful and wise. But the very day before our marriage the Governor of Mosul remembered my country and invaded it with a thousand men. And little enough plunder they got from our village, but they caught Pervaneh walking alone among the pine woods and carried her away. When I heard this I leapt on my horse and galloped to Mosul, prepared to slay the Governor and all the inhabitants thereof single-handed, if evil had come to Pervaneh. But there I found she had already been sent with a raft full of slaves down the Tigris to Bagdad. Whereupon I hired six men with shining muscles to row me there. We arrived at Bagdad at the end of the third night's rowing at the grey of dawn. I sprang out of the raft like a tiger, and ran like a madman through the streets, crying 'The Slave Market! Tell me the way, O ye citizens! The Slave Market, O the Slave Market!'

And suddenly turning a corner I came upon the market, which was like a garden full of girls in splendid clothes grouped in groups like flowers in garden beds and some like lilies, naked. I ran round the market to find Pervaneh and all the women laughed at me aloud, and behold there she stood; she who had never worn a veil before, the only veiled woman in all the market, for she had sworn to bite off her lips if her master would not veil her: but I knew her by the beauty of her hands, and I cried: 'O dealer, the veiled woman for a thousand

49

dinars!' And the dealer laughed in the way of dea lers a
the presumption of my offer and demanded two
thousand, and so I purchased for gold the blood of my
own heart, and she lifted her veil and sang for joy and
hung upon my neck, and all the slave girls clapped their
hands.

But at that moment there entered the market a negro
eunuch, so tall and so disgusting that the sun was
darkened, and the birds whistled for terror in the trees.
And all the dealers and the slaves bowed low before him.
Coming to my dealer, he cried: 'Why dost thou sell
slaves before the Caliph has made his choice?'

Then turning to Pervaneh, he said, 'Go back to thy
place.' And I cried, 'She is my purchase.' But the
eunuch said, 'Hold thy peace; I take her for the Caliph.'
And suddenly two guards seized Pervaneh, and I drawing my sword was about to hew the eunuch into a
thousand pieces, but Pervaneh made a sign to me, and
looking up I saw I was surrounded by men at arms. And
Pervaneh cried in the speech of my country, as they
carried her away: 'I will die, but I will not be defiled:
rescue me alive or dead, soon or late, and avenge me on
this Caliph, may the ravens eat his entrails!'

That is my story, and for this reason I will nail the
Caliph down in his coffin, bound and living and with
open eyes.

CALIPH (*in horror*): Bound and living, with open eyes!
Thou devil!

MASRUR: Is that all the story?

JAFAR: Will you tear up the Empire for the honour of a
girl?

CALIPH (*in fury*): And set your worthless passion in scale
against the splendour of Islam!

Rafi: Is this Haroun the splendour of Islam? Is the prosperity of his people, a rosy slave in his serai, or their happiness, a fish in his silver fountain?

Jafar: God will frustrate thee.

Rafi: If He will. Farewell, my guests. I go to avenge Pervaneh, and to wash Bagdad in blood.

Jafar: And what of us?

Rafi: It is well for you that you are my guests, for you are rich and proud, and eminently deserve destruction. But you are as safe in this room as in an iron cage; you will only hear, as in a dream, the crash of the fall of the statue of tyranny.

Caliph (*rushing to intercept him*): By the thick smoke of Hell's Pit and the Ghouls that eat men's flesh, you shall not go, and we shall not stay.

Rafi: Look twice before you touch me!

(*He leaps behind the archway. The* Beggars *and the* Women *are now lined close to the wall of the room and the* Guests *are isolated in the centre. From behind every pillar appears an* Archer *with bow drawn taut directed on the startled* Guests.)

Chorus of Beggars and Dancing Girls:
> To-day the fools who catch a cold in summer
> > Will fly for winter in the windy moon.
> To-day the little rills of shining water
> > Will catch the fire of morning oversoon.
> To-day the state musicians and court poets
> > Will set new verses to a special tune.
> To-day Haroun, the much-detested Caliph
> > Will find his Caliphate inopportune.

Rafi (*silencing the* Singers *with a wave of his hand; to the* Guests): Did not someone ask me why this house was called the House of the Moving Walls?

CALIPH: I asked the question.

(*Sheets of iron fall with a crash covering the apertures of the arches. The* FOUR GUESTS *are completely walled in.*)

RAFI, BEGGARS AND WOMEN (*from behind the iron partitions with a shout*): Answered!

JAFAR: This is a disastrous situation!

(*The* BEGGARS *tramp out to martial music.*)

VOICES OF THE BEGGARS (*retreating*):

> To-day Haroun, the much-detested Caliph,
> Will find his Caliphate inopportune!

JAFAR (*listening at the wall*): They have all left the room. At least we are alone. Let us shout, they may hear us from the street.

MASRUR (*banging on the wall*): Eyyah! Help, help, men of Bagdad! The Caliph is in danger! The Caliph is in prison! ... Come up and save the Caliph, the Master of Men, the Shaker of the World! ...

(*Silence.*)

CALIPH: There comes no answering cheer ...

JAFAR: I had forgotten the height of this room above the streets: and on either side stretches the empty garden of this house!

(*The* CALIPH, JAFAR *and* MASRUR *rush round as though trying to find a way out of their prison, and banging on the iron walls.* HASSAN *takes his seat on the carpet.*)

CALIPH: Allah! and this room is a box within a box like a Chinese toy. And that man will surprise my soldiers in the chill of dawn, and sack my palace and burn Bagdad. He will discover my identity and bury me alive!

JAFAR: Alas, Master! What shall we do?

CALIPH: Thou dog! Thou dirt! Thou dunghill! Thou dustheap! Did I make thee Vizier to ask counsel or to give it? Find out what we shall do! Thou hast let me fall into a trap, and now dost quiver and quake and shiver and shake like a tub of whey on the back of a restive camel: my kingdom is reduced from twelve provinces to twelve square cubits: my subjects from thirty millions unto three, but, Bismillah! one of my subjects is the Executioner, and Mashallah! another one merits execution: and Inshallah! if thy head doth not immediately devise a practicable scheme of escape it shall dive off thy shoulders and swim across the floor.

JAFAR: What shall happen, shall happen. But here is one who is occupied in meditation, and is aloof from the circumstances of the moment: let us invite him to Council.

CALIPH: Ho, thou Hassan! What occupies thy spirit?

HASSAN: I am examining the square of carpet. It is of cheap manufacture, inferior dye and unpleasant pattern.

CALIPH: Art thou a carpet dealer?

HASSAN: No, sir, I am a confectioner.

CALIPH: And I am the Caliph.

HASSAN: As my heart surmised. O Commander of the Faithful! (*Performs the ceremonies prescribed.*)

CALIPH: Canst thou give me one gleam of hope of salvation, Hassan, the Confectioner? If not, Masrur shall cut off all our heads, beginning with thine. I dare not fall into that man's hands alive.

HASSAN: But I dare! O spare me, spare me! What of the man who put me in the basket? He will know where we are, and come to our rescue.

CALIPH: No good – no good. I would rather depend on the mercy of Rafi than on the whim of Ishak. Masrur, unsheathe. There is no hope.

HASSAN: Thy pardon on thy servant: there is hope! Behold the light!

(Points to crack between bottom of the iron wall and floor towards the balcony.)

CALIPH: By the seven lakes of Hell, we are not mice!

HASSAN: A mouse could not pass. But what, O Master, of a message?

CALIPH: A message?

HASSAN: Written out black on paper, and dropped into the street.

CALIPH: Ho, Jafar, thou art a fool to this man! Take out thy pen and write. Warn the Captain of the Soldiers. Warn the Police. Describe our position. Offer the Government of Three Provinces to the man who picks up the paper. Write clearly, write quicker. Time's flying. Write, and we are saved. Write for the Salvation of Bagdad; write for the safety of Islam! O Hassan, the Confectioner, if we are rescued I will fill thy mouth with gold!

(JAFAR having written on a long roll of paper, they thrust it in the crack.)

HASSAN: No: at the corner here, where there is no balcony and the wall drops straight into the street.

(MASRUR pokes out the paper with his sword.)

CALIPH: And now how shall we employ the time of waiting for our deliverance?

JAFAR: I shall meditate upon the mutability of human affairs.

MASRUR: And I shall sharpen my sword upon my thigh.

HASSAN: And I shall study the reasons of the excessive ugliness of the pattern of this carpet.

CALIPH: Hassan, I will join thee: thou art a man of taste.

54

(See ACT I, *last Scene)*

Again the street outside the house — the Street of the Fountain, with the balcony of RAFI *and the balcony of* YASMIN *opposite. Cold light before dawn.*

(On the steps of the Fountain, two tired MENDICANTS *asleep. One slowly rubs his eyes and looks round him. A paper comes floating down. One tired* MAN *lazily catches it.)*

FIRST LOITERER: Here comes a new chapter of the Koran falling down from Heaven.

SECOND LOITERER: Is it written, Abdu?

ABDU: It is written, Ali.

ALI: Read what is written, Abdu.

ABDU: I cannot read. Am I a schoolmaster?

(Folds paper, puts it in his belt, and prepares to sleep again. Several interesting ORIENTALS *pass by.)*

ALI: Abdu!

ABDU: I sleep.

ALI: I can read: give me the paper.

ABDU: I am asleep: get up and take it from my belt if you want it, Ya Ali, I am heavy with great sleep, like a tortoise in November.

ALI: Ya Abdu, I am too languishing to move. It is a paper and it is written. It does not matter. To-morrow or the next day it will be read.

ABDU: To-morrow or the next day I shall wake and pass it to you.

(Interval: more interesting ORIENTALS *go by.)*

ALI *(with sudden inspiration)*: Blow me the paper, Abdu.

ABDU: Alas, Allah sent thee to trouble the world!

*(*ABDU *blows the paper over.* ALI *with infinite difficulty spells it out, murmuring:)*

55

ALI: Ha, alif, alif re wow wow 'ain jeem – ah, ye blessed ones in Paradise, is it thus ye write a jeem? Nun – but art thou a nun, O letter, or a drunkard's qaf? Verily an ape has written this with his tail: I have the second line. (*With a start.*) Ho, Abdu, whence came this? Do not pretend to sleep. Answer me.

ABDU: From the sky: how do I know?

ALI: Let me look at the sky. (*Rolls on his back and stares upward.*) I tell you, Abdu, a mighty joker has flung this from the balcony.

ABDU: Allah plague him and his pen and thee! Is there no peace in the world?

ALI: Here it is written, and do thou listen, O Abdu, for this is the strangest of the strange writings that are strange: 'Whoever findeth this paper, know that the Caliph is in the house above, a prisoner, and his friends prisoners, and in the extremity of danger, he and they, with all Bagdad. Let the rescue be swift and sudden, but above all secret. The iron walls must be lifted from beneath. And send a man at once to the Guard, O fortunate discoverer, to warn them to protect the palace against the Beggars of Bagdad, and thou shalt be made Governor of Three Provinces. Signed, Jafar, the Vizier.' (*Bursting into laughter.*) Three Provinces, well I know their Three Provinces! Some rich young reveller hopes to play a game with poor old Ali, even as a game was played on the son of Abdallah, whom they dressed as a woman and placed in the Grand Vizier's Harem, and his reward came hailing down on his toes. (*In a lower voice.*) And I tell you, Abdu, what if the Caliph were in the house and his friends? What if this were true? Who would believe me? Who am I to rescue the Caliph? I never meddle in politics.

ABDU: May the great gripes settle on thee and on the
Caliph and the mother of the Caliph. Shall I not sleep?
And now there comes a disturbance down the road. Ya,
Jehannum, the Police!

(CHIEF OF POLICE *with* ISHAK.)

ISHAK: I tell you, I do not know precisely where I left
them. It was night. It was somewhere in this quarter.
It may have been this balcony they went to or that, but
there are a thousand balconies. It was above a fountain,
but there are a million fountains. I tell you they always
come back. Have you not already twenty such scares as
these for the safety of the Caliph?

CHIEF OF POLICE: Never and on no preceding occasion
has his exalted name been so long delayed in his return
to the palace. The day is dawning.

ISHAK: I tell you, if you do find him you will get no
thanks, O man of arms. Will you dare to unstick the
Ruler of the Moslem World from the embrace of his
latest slave girl or dash the cup of pleasure from his
reluctant hand?

CHIEF OF POLICE: I tell you, if you do not find him,
O man of letters, I will have you impaled upon a monstrous pen.

(Seizes him.)

ISHAK: Thou beastly, blood-drinking brute and bloated
bully, take off thy stable-reeking hands.

CHIEF OF POLICE: Yallah, these poets. They talk in
rhyme.

ALI (*who has risen and salaamed, advancing*): I pray you,
Sirs, ...

CHIEF OF POLICE: O thou maggot! Darest thou address
us?

ALI: I pray you only regard ...

57

CHIEF OF POLICE: I pray you only remove, or I will split you from the top.

ISHAK: Do you not see that he has a paper, and that his manners are superior to yours, O Captain of Police? Let me look at thy paper. ... Ah – ah. Whence came this, O virtuous wanderer?

ALI: From that balcony, may thy slave be forgiven!

CHIEF OF POLICE: This is a very important clue. Let us break in the door.

ISHAK: There is no door. But first of all send word to the Palace Guard.

CHIEF OF POLICE (*to a soldier*): Ali. (*To the other* ALI, *who runs and says:* Excellence, I hear and obey.) Not thou, fool. Did Allah make the name Ali for thee alone? Who art thou that I should address thee? Are there not ten thousand Alis in Bagdad, and wilt thou lift up thy head, O worm, when I say Ali? (*To* POLICE-MAN.) Here is my ring. Take this paper, and run with all thy might and show it to the Captain of the Palace guard.

POLICEMAN: I hear and obey. (*Starts off.*)

ISHAK (*stopping him*): Wait!

CHIEF OF POLICE: What right have you to stop my man, you bastard son of a quill-bearing barn-fowl?

ISHAK: Since when had a bludgeoning policeman the practical good sense of a thought-breathing poet? Tell them, Ali, to send a few men with levers and ladders.

CHIEF OF POLICE: It is well ordered: run, run, Ali!

ISHAK: You other Ali, who brought the paper ...

ALI: Master?

ISHAK: How long is it since any paper was thrown from the balcony?

ALI: How do I know time? The time to go to market and buy a melon.

CHIEF OF POLICE: By the great pit of torment, this swine-faced has had the paper a good hour! By the red blaze of damnation, thou maggot, why didst thou not run with this at once to the Palace Guard?

ALI: I had a great fear, and I thought it was a jest.

CHIEF OF POLICE: A jest! Rivers of blood, a jest! The life of the Caliph of Bagdad, a jest! The safety of the Empire a jest! I knew thee a traitor from thy face. I will teach thee jesting. I will teach thee fear. Ho, Mahmud, Zia, Rustem, down with his head and up with his heels.

ALI (*as his feet are looped into the pole to receive the bastinado*): Ya, Abdu, you had the letter first, it is yours. Will you not claim it and the reward? Alas, that the Governor of Three Provinces should be treated thus!

ABDU: Do I meddle in politics? Hit him hard, O executioner, for he is a great disturber of peaceful citizens. But as for me, O Ali, lest my sleep be troubled by thy groaning, I will make my way a little further on. (*Exit.*)

(*The* EXECUTIONERS *proceed with their work, but stop on entrance of* CAPTAIN OF THE MILITARY *with* SOLDIERS.)

(*On the balcony opposite house where* CALIPH *is imprisoned appears* YASMIN.)

YASMIN: Look, look, Selim! there's a man being beaten.

SELIM: Come in quick! this is a riot or some trouble; come in quick, and shut the shutters fast.

YASMIN: You are a valiant protection indeed for frail-as-a-rose ladies in danger's hour!

(*They remain at the window.*)

CAPTAIN OF MILITARY (*to* CHIEF OF POLICE): Sir.

CHIEF OF POLICE: Sir.

CAPTAIN OF MILITARY (*saluting*): Captain of the Victorious Army, at your service!

CHIEF OF POLICE (*saluting*): Chief of the August Police, at yours.

CAPTAIN OF MILITARY (*bowing*): I am honoured.

CHIEF OF POLICE (*bowing*): I am overwhelmed.

ISHAK: Come, Sirs, brush away, I implore you, the cobwebs of ceremony with the broom of expedition.

CHIEF OF POLICE: Sir, when men of action meet, the place of the man of letters is inside his pencase.

CAPTAIN OF MILITARY: A moment! Ere we proceed, Chief of Police, may I ask why this man is undergoing punishment?

CHIEF OF POLICE: Since your excellency deigns to enquire, for urgent reasons of police.

CAPTAIN OF MILITARY: They must have been very urgent indeed before you would permit such an inopportune disturbance outside the very house where our Lord the Caliph is imprisoned. You have seriously impaired our chances of a speedy and effective rescue.

CHIEF OF POLICE (*drawing his sword and whirling it about*): Thou melon head, thou dung pig, thou brother of disaster, get thee hence with thy knock-kneed band of fatherless brigands, ere I have thee arrested for unnatural crime.

CAPTAIN OF MILITARY: Out with thy sword, thou big-bellied snatcher up of burglars, thou manacler of little boys, thou terror of the peaceful market. I will teach thee to insult the slaughterers of the infidel host.

ISHAK (*intercepting the* COMBATANTS): Is this a time for indecent brawling? Quick, where are the ladders?

A SOLDIER (*pompously*): In the rear, Sir, in the rear.

(The ladders are brought along.)

CHIEF OF POLICE *(to* POLICEMAN*)*: Place a ladder.

CAPTAIN OF MILITARY *(to* SOLDIERS*)*: Place a ladder.

(Each goes up his ladder at the same time: bang at the iron wall and are answered: shout for levers which are procured, and assistance which speedily arrives. The iron wall is lifted up, and CALIPH *and the* REST *disclosed seated peaceably awaiting their deliverance, the lamp still burning.)*

CHIEF OF POLICE: My royal master!

CAPTAIN OF MILITARY: August Lord.

CHIEF AND CAPTAIN *(together)*: I have saved thee, Master.

(Each attempts to seize the CALIPH.*)*

CHIEF OF POLICE: Honourable Police! ...

CAPTAIN OF MILITARY: Honourable Military! ...

CHIEF OF POLICE: It has been the high privilege of this grovelling slave to rescue the Lamp of the World. I shall carry him down.

CAPTAIN OF MILITARY: Permit me to observe, O fire-spitting Battle Cleaver, that I was first up this ladder, and though I tremble to obscure the Sun's Brilliance with my dirty hand, yet it is I who have the prior claim.

*(*MASRUR *pushes them aside, and assists the* CALIPH *down the ladder.* JAFAR *and* HASSAN *follow. Shouts of 'Long live the Caliph' from all the people gathered in the street. The* SOLDIERS *salute. The* CALIPH *raises his hand. Silence.)*

CALIPH: Is my Palace safe?

MASRUR: O Lord and Master, we pray so.

CALIPH: And my people?

JAFAR: Around thee, O Lord and Master.

YASMIN *(from her balcony)*: By the Prophet, here is Hassan with the Caliph!

CALIPH: Are we all saved?

MASRUR: All, by the providence of Allah.

JAFAR: And the wisdom of Hassan.

CALIPH: And the Guard warned?

CAPTAIN OF MILITARY: All warned and at their posts, my Lord.

CALIPH: Allah, deliver our enemies into their hands! Let Hassan come before me.

HASSAN (*prostrating himself*): Master!

CALIPH (*raising him*): Rise, Hassan. This Hassan, yesterday a stranger, has to-night by his skill and invention, saved my life and rescued this city from a greater peril than my death.

CROWD: May it be far!

CALIPH: Therefore here and now, in the presence of all, I nominate Hassan to my court, to hold rank among my subjects second to none save to Jafar, my Grand Vizier.

YASMIN (*who has been at her balcony with* SELIM): O Allah!

CROWD: Honour to Hassan. Honour to Hassan.

HASSAN: Master, I sold confectionery in the market.

JAFAR: Thou shalt now confection the sweets of prosperity.

ISHAK (*to* HASSAN): Why, Hassan! You are the man with the broken lute.

CALIPH: Is that the voice of Ishak?

ISHAK: It is the voice of Ishak that has often sung to you.

CALIPH: Why did you abandon me, Ishak, and flee into the night? I do not know if I shall forgive you.

ISHAK: I was weary of you, Haroun-ar-Raschid.

CALIPH: And if I weary of you?

ISHAK: You will one day or another, and you will have me slain.

CALIPH: And what of this day that dawns?

ISHAK: Dawn is the hour when most men die.

CALIPH: Your death is granted you, Ishak; you have but to kneel.

(*A red glow on the horizon.*)

ISHAK (*as he kneels calmly*): Why have they pinned the carpet of execution on the sky?

MASRUR: It is the Caliph's dawn.

JAFAR: Thy dawn, O Master!

ISHAK:

Thy dawn, O Master of the world, thy dawn;
The hour the lilies open on the lawn,
The hour the grey wings pass beyond the mountains,
The hour of silence, when we hear the fountains,
The hour that dreams are brighter and winds colder,
The hour that young love wakes on a white shoulder,
O Master of the world, the Persian Dawn.

That hour, O Master, shall be bright for thee:
Thy merchants chase the morning down the sea,
The braves who fight thy war unsheathe the sabre,
The slaves who work thy mines are lashed to labour,
For thee the waggons of the world are drawn —
The ebony of night, the red of dawn!

CALIPH: Sheathe your sword, Masrur! Would you kill my friend?

MASRUR: I hear and obey.

CALIPH: I must go swiftly to my palace. But to you, Ishak, I leave the care of this man you sent up to me in the basket, who has proved the salvation of Bagdad. Teach him the ceremonies and regulations. Is my chair ready?

BEARERS: Ready, Lord and Master.

(*Exit* CALIPH *in* chair, *and* JAFAR *and* CROWD;

ISHAK *signs to those who would kiss* HASSAN's *feet to leave him.*)

YASMIN (*on balcony opposite. Giving* SELIM *a great clout on the ear*): Go, leave my sight, you fool. I shall burst with fury. You made me insult Hassan, and now he is going to court.

SELIM (*astonished*): Eh, Yasmin, Yasmin, how could I know?

ISHAK: Ah, bismillah, I had not forgotten you, O man with the broken lute.

HASSAN: The broken lute? The broken lute?

ISHAK: Here you were lying, at this fountain, like one dead.

HASSAN: Was it here? Is that the balcony? Who are you? Why do you mock me? What do you know?

ISHAK: Quietly, friend, quietly, your head is weak with joy.

HASSAN: With joy? Do I know what is true or false? Do I know if the Caliph is the Caliph? And if the Caliph is the Caliph may he not mock me too? What is joy? Let me look at that balcony for joy. I dare not look, I fear she is there. Ah, it is she!

(YASMIN *takes the rose from her hair and flings it at* HASSAN, *then retires within.*)

ISHAK: Are you fortunate in love as well as in life, O Hassan? But come away. This conduct ill beseems a minister of state; you are not unobserved.

HASSAN: I am coming. The rose is poisoned.

ISHAK: O friend, is this talk for the ardent lover?

HASSAN: Are you my friend? You, Ishak, the glorious singer of Islam! And if you are my friend, are you like those who were my friends before?

ISHAK: Last night, I found you lying like a filthy corpse

64

beneath this window, but I knew by your lute and your countenance that you were a poet, like myself, and I was sorry to think you dead.

HASSAN: A poet? I? I am a confectioner.

ISHAK: You are my friend, Hassan.

HASSAN: Then consider this rose. This rose is more bitter than colocynth. For look you, friend, had she not flung this rose, I would have said she hated me and loved another; it is well. She had the right to hate and love. She could hate and she could love. But now, ah, tell me, you who seem to be a friend, are all you poets liars?

ISHAK: Ya, Hassan, but we tell excellent lies.

HASSAN: Why do you say that beauty has a meaning? Why do you not say that beauty is as hollow as a drum? Why do you not say it is sold?

ISHAK: All this disillusionment because a fair lady flung you a rose!

HASSAN: Last night I baked sugar and she flung me water: this morning I bake gold and she flings me a rose. Empty, empty, I tell you, friend, all the blue sky.

ISHAK: Come, forget her and come away. I will instruct you in the pleasures of the court.

HASSAN: Forget, forget? O rose of morning and O rose of evening, vainly for me shall you fade on domes of ebony or azure. This rose has faded, and this rose is bitter, and this rose is nothing but the world.

CURTAIN

ACT III

The garden of the CALIPH'S *palace: in front of a pavilion.
The* CALIPH: HASSAN *in fine raiment, a sword of honour at
his side.*

CALIPH: Yes, what the chief Eunuch told you is all true,
my Hassan. Our late host, the King of the Beggars, was
captured hiding in the gutter of his roof. This evening
I shall judge him and his crew in full divan. And in the
divan shalt thou appear, O Hassan, clothed in thy robe
of ceremony, and seated on my right hand.

HASSAN: Alas, O Serene Splendour, thy servant is a man
of humble origin and limited desires. I am one who
would obey the old poet's behest:

> *Give all thy day to dreaming and all thy night to sleep:
> Let not Ambition's Tyger devour Contentment's Sheep!*

I am not one to open my mouth at divans, or to strut
among courtiers in robes of state. Sir, excuse me from
these things. Dispose thy favour like a high golden wall,
and protect the life of thy servant from the wind of
complication. But at evening, when God flings roses
through the sky, call me then to some calm pavilion,
and let us hear Ishak play and let us hear Ishak sing, till
you forget you are Lord of all the World, and I forget
that I am a baseborn tradesman; till we discover the
speech of things that have no life, and know what the
clods of earth are saying to the roots of the garden trees.

66

CALIPH: Have no fear. You shall inhabit the place I shall assign you in untroubled peace, and meditate till your beard grows into the soil and you become wiser than Aflatun. But in this case you are a witness and must be present at my divan, be it but for this once only. And you shall call me Emir of the Faithful, Redresser of Wrong, the Shadow of Good on Earth, and Peacock of the World. But in this garden you are Hassan, and I am your friend Haroun, and you must address me as a friend.

HASSAN (*kissing* CALIPH'S *hand*): O master, you speak gently, but I must fear you all the more.

CALIPH: But why? I am but a kindly man. I love single-heartedness in men as I love simplicity in my palace. There you have seen floors with but one carpet – but that carpet like a meadow. You have seen walls with but one curtain – but that curtain a sunset on the sea. You have seen white rooms all naked marble: but they await my courtiers all clothed like flowers. If, therefore, I avoid complexity in the matter of walls and floors, shall I not be simple in the things of heart and soul? Shall I not, Hassan, be just your friend?

HASSAN: Master, I find thy friendship like thy palace, endowed with all the charm of beauty and the magic of surprise. As thou knowest, I am but a man of the streets of Bagdad, and there men say, 'The Caliph's Palace, Mashallah! The walls are stiff with gold and the ceilings plated with silver, and the urinals thereof are lined with turquoise blue.' And hearing men say this, many a time hath Hassan the Confectioner stroked the chin of Hassan the Confectioner saying, 'O Hassan, thy back parlour is less ugly than that, with its tub for boiling sugar, and one good Bokhara carpet hanging on the wall. And twelve months did I work at the tub, boiling sugar to buy that carpet.'

CALIPH: What a man you are for poetry and carpets! When you tread on a carpet, you drop your eyes to earth to catch the pattern and when you hear a poem, you raise your eyes to heaven to hear the tune. Whoever saw a confectioner like this! When did you learn poetry, Hassan of my heart?

HASSAN: In that great school, the Market of Bagdad. For thee, Master of the World, poetry is a princely diversion, but for us it was a deliverance from Hell. Allah made poetry a cheap thing to buy and a simple thing to understand. He gave men dreams by night that they might learn to dream by day. Men who work hard have special need of these dreams. All the town of Bagdad is passionate for poetry, O Master. Dost thou not know what great crowds gather to hear the epic of Antari sung in the streets at evening? I have seen cobblers weep and butchers bury their great faces in their hands!

CALIPH: By Eblis and the powers of Hell, should I not know this, and know that therein lies the secret of the strength of Islam? In poems and in tales alone shall live the eternal memory of this city when I am dust and thou art dust, when the Bedouin shall build his hut upon my garden and drive his plough beyond the ruins of my palace, and all Bagdad is broken to the ground. Ah, if there shall ever arise a nation whose people have forgotten poetry or whose poets have forgotten the people, though they send their ships round Taprobane and their armies across the hills of Hindustan, though their city be greater than Babylon of old, though they mine a league into earth or mount to the stars on wings – what of them?

HASSAN: They will be a dark patch upon the world.

CALIPH: Well said! By your luck you have saved the life of the Caliph, O Hassan; but by your conversation you have won the friendship of Haroun. Indeed — but at what are you gazing as if enchanted?

HASSAN: What a beautiful fountain, with the silver dolphin and the naked boy.

CALIPH: A Greek of Constantinople made it, who came travelling hither in the days of my father, the Caliph El Madhi (may earth be gentle to his body and Paradise refreshing to his soul!). He showed this fountain to my father, who was exceptionally pleased, and asked the Greek if he could make more as fine. 'A hundred,' replied the delighted infidel. Whereupon my father cried, 'Impale this pig.' Which having been done, this fountain remains the loveliest in the world.

HASSAN (*with anguish*): O Fountain, dost thou never run with blood?

CALIPH: Why, what is the matter, Hassan?

HASSAN: You have told a tale of death and tyranny, O Master of the World.

CALIPH (*in a sudden and towering rage*): Do you accuse my father of tyranny, O fellow, for slaying a filthy Christian?

HASSAN (*prostrating himself*): I meant no offence. My life is at your feet. But you bade me talk to you as a friend.

CALIPH: Not Ishak, not Ishak himself, who has been my friend for years, would dare address me thus. (*Bursting into laughter.*) Rise, Hassan. Thy impudence hath a monstrous beauty, like the hindquarters of an elephant.

HASSAN: Forgive me, forgive me.

CALIPH: I forgive you with all my heart, but, I advise you, speak in conformity with your character and of things you understand, and never leave the Garden of Art for the Palace of Action. Trouble not your head with the tyranny of Princes, or you may catch a cold therein from the Wind of Complication. Keep to your poetry and carpets, Hassan, and make no reference to politics, for which even the market of Bagdad is an insufficient school.

HASSAN (*dolefully*): I hear and obey.

CALIPH: Forget it now; set your mind on pleasant things. Have you noticed this little pavilion in front of which we have talked so long? This is your little house, good Hassan, where you shall find a shelter from the wind you so much dislike and all other blasts that harm or chill.

HASSAN: My little house?

CALIPH: I chose it for you, knowing your disposition. Here in this remote corner of the garden you will hear no noise of street or palace, but enjoy complete repose.

HASSAN (*with rapture*): Mine, this little house? Mine, this sweet-scented door!

CALIPH: Knock on it and see.

(HASSAN *knocks. The door opens and* ALDER, WILLOW, JUNIPER, *and* TAMARISK *appear.* TAMARISK, *the youngest, has somewhat of a mouse's squeak.*)

ALDER (*to* CALIPH *with prostration*): O Emir of the Faithful!

WILLOW (*to* CALIPH *with prostration*): O Redresser of Wrong!

JUNIPER (*to* CALIPH *with prostration*): O Shadow of God on Earth!

TAMARISK (*to* CALIPH *with prostration*): O Peacock of the World!

ALDER (*to* HASSAN *with prostration*): Master!

WILLOW (*to* HASSAN *with prostration*): Master!

JUNIPER (*to* HASSAN *with prostration*): Master!

TAMARISK (*to* HASSAN *with prostration*): Master!

(*They stand, their hands in their sleeves, across the doorway.*)

HASSAN: But these are the slaves of the King of the Beggars, who bathed me, anointed me, and brought back my soul into my eyes, whence a woman had all but driven it for ever.

CALIPH: I have rescued them from the ruin of their master's house as their polite and finished manners deserve, and I have given them to you since you are likely to need and appreciate their service.

HASSAN: And so faces not altogether strange shall welcome me to my home. (*Kneels and kisses* CALIPH'S *hand.*)

CALIPH: Say not a word. For the pen of happiness hath written on thy face the ode of gratitude. (*To* SLAVES.) Is all ready?

ALDER (*pompously*): Ready, O Gardener of the Vale of Islam.

WILLOW: Prepared, O Lion. ...

CALIPH: Enough! Conduct your master into his house, show him all there is inside, and serve him faithfully. Enter with them, Hassan; delicious has been our converse, but Jafar, the Vizier, has been awaiting me some two hours. (*As* HASSAN *is about to prostrate himself.*) No, it is thus Haroun takes leave of his friends.

(*Kisses him on both cheeks.* HASSAN *watches till he is out of sight, pensive. Then he goes to the fountain and observes it a moment. Then he advances slowly to the folding door of the pavilion which* ALDER *and* WILLOW *hold open for him.*)

ALDER: Fortunate be thy entry!

WILLOW: Prosperous thy sojourn!

JUNIPER: Quiet thy days!

TAMARISK: And riotous thy nights!

SCENE II

The private apartment within the pavilion. A bed. Fine furniture. A window with a view on the garden.

(*Enter* HASSAN *followed by his* SLAVES.)

HASSAN: In that apartment, therefore, I shall receive guests. But in this apartment, whom?

ALDER: Such ladies, Master, as you desire to honour.

HASSAN: Yes, yes. I must visit the market and see. (*Staring at the floor, with a start.*) Wulluhi, what is that?

TAMARISK: The carpet, Master.

HASSAN: One of the wonderful new carpets of Ispahan. A hunting scene. The Prince. His followers. Leopards and stags and three tigers, and an elephant – his head only. O amazing carpet. And everywhere great scarlet flowers, very stiff and fine. O exquisite carpet. I have never seen so bright a scarlet. (*With a sudden earnestness.*) Tell me. You were his slaves ...?

ALDER: Master?

HASSAN: Well, well, we will not talk of it. How clearly that fountain sounds outside with its little splash!

ALDER: I pray you, Master. The Caliph said you should particularly observe this mirror with the carven frame.

HASSAN (*looking at himself*): By the Prophet, what a Phœnix I have become! Provided I do not stumble on my sword.

WILLOW: The Caliph hoped you should not fail to remark this exquisitely upholstered couch.

JUNIPER: The Caliph hoped you would admire these toilet requisites in alabaster.

TAMARISK: The Caliph hopes you will make good use of this very slender whip for our correction.

HASSAN: A whip? For your correction, O slaves of charm? Am I the man to spoil good almond paste with streaks of cochineal?

ALDER: Thou art pleased, O my Master?

HASSAN: Pleased? Look at the acacia tapping at my window; one night it will come in softly and fling its moonlit blossom at my feet. But this is no place for a man to live alone. Without a doubt I must visit the market. They have Circassians; I have always wanted a Circassian. She must be very young. ... I have not finished the excellencies of the room. These three chests, what do they contain?

ALDER: This chest, O Master, contains your new robes. One of them is embroidered with red carnations and silver bells.

HASSAN: Was there ever generosity like this!

WILLOW: This chest, O Master, contains curtains, hangings, and cushions for the sofa. One of the cushions is embellished with fifteen peacocks.

HASSAN: Fifteen peacocks! And all those peacocks dumb!

JUNIPER: This chest, O Master, contains fresh linen for your bed. All marked with your name.

HASSAN: Marked with my name! And what have you to say, Tamarisk?

TAMARISK: That bed ...

HASSAN: That bed is not a chest. But doubtless it also contains fresh linen marked with my name.

TAMARISK (*tremulous*): That bed contains a most beautiful lady.

HASSAN (*jumping*): What?

TAMARISK: A most beautiful lady. She said she must see you, and gave me ten dinars.

YASMIN (*as* HASSAN *tears aside the curtains of the bed*): Hassan!

(*She is dressed in a cloak and veiled.*)

HASSAN: What voice?

YASMIN: Hassan. (*She unveils.*)

HASSAN: Thou!

YASMIN: I came: I hid: I waited.

HASSAN: Why?

YASMIN: Why does a woman hide in the bed of a man?

HASSAN (*furiously*.): You dared! Stay here, slaves. Will you leave me at this moment, you fools who let this woman in? (*To* YASMIN.) You dared?

YASMIN: What is there a beautiful woman dare not dare?

HASSAN: But your impudence is vile. Out of it! Get you back to Selim.

YASMIN: I have left Selim.

HASSAN: Left Selim to come to me?

YASMIN: I found Selim a coward and a fool. I have discovered in you a man of taste and valour. How could I have known before? But what matter? Am I not white enough to follow the caravans of Wealth and Power? (*Flinging out her arms.*) Is this for Selim or that for Selim?

HASSAN: Back to him, and no more words! You darken the world before my eyes. If he is a fool and a coward, you are nothing but a whore. Go, or my slaves shall fling you head foremost down my steps.

YASMIN: I have left Selim because he proved a coward, a fool, a poor man and a nobody. I have come to you because you are rich, famous, and a man of taste. The

74

day you fall into disfavour (may it be far, O my master!) I shall undoubtedly leave you. Till that day you will find me faithful. I am that which you call me — but I bring you a fair merchandise.

HASSAN: I thank you, O seller of yourself. I buy no tainted meat. I beg you seek another market, and that extremely soon.

YASMIN (*rubbing her face and rising lightly*): I did not know I had a taint, O Master. The mirror must deceive me. But merchandise must be well inspected before its inferiority is assured. It must be seen and touched. Will you see and will you touch?

HASSAN (*stepping back*): Oh, away, away! Why did you seek me out? Is it to rain back my words upon my face? Or do you hope once more to show me yourself limb after limb in the embrace of a new Selim? I pray you, however, spare the water from the jug. My fire needs no quenching.

YASMIN (*suppliant*): Be generous. It beseems the Caliph's friend to be generous. If I have made you jealous, do I not offer you a sumptuous revenge?

HASSAN: Rise, take your pardon, and depart. Shall I tell you again? If you need money, the slaves will give it you at the door.

YASMIN: You are as cold as ice.

HASSAN: You are brazen.

YASMIN: I am brave. Farewell, I see you are not a man of love.

HASSAN: Farewell. And defile no more the word love with your painted lips.

YASMIN (*lingering at the door*): Yet there is little of love's language that I do not know. When the bird of night sings on the bough of the tree that rustles outside your

75

window, and the shadows creep away from the moon across the floor, I could have sung you a song sweeter than the nightingales and shown you a whiteness whiter than the moon.

HASSAN: Ah – go!

YASMIN: Because I was cruel could I not be kind? Because you can buy my body, can you buy my soul? Because I am of the people have I no songs to sing? Because I have sinned have I no secret to impart? Go to market, O Hassan, and buy your Circassian girl. And one day you shall say: Had Yasmin but lied to me of love, it were better than this fool's sincerity.

HASSAN: Ah, leave me!

YASMIN: There are lilies by the thousand in the meadows: there are roses by the thousand in the gardens, and all as like as like – but there is only one shape in the world like mine. There is only one face in the world where these eyebrows arch and these eyes flash – where the nostrils are set just so, and the lips are parted thus. There is no other arm beneath the sky that has here this curve and here this dimple, and here the light soft golden hairs. There are rows and rows of young fair girls in the Caliph's harem and many as fair as I, but none whose veins are these veins, whose flesh is this flesh, fiery and cool, whose body swings like mine upon the heel. (*Flinging off her cloak.*) Will you see and will you touch? (*Approaching.*) Will you see and will you touch? (*Putting her arm round his neck.*) Will you touch?

HASSAN (*with a shout as he pushes her back*): Slaves, tear off this woman!

YASMIN (*as the* SLAVES *force her back*): Eh, your slaves are violent!

HASSAN (*to* SLAVES): Hold her!

76

YASMIN: But you must let me go.

HASSAN: I will not let you go.

YASMIN: Come, I see you are but a sour fellow, for whom pleasure is but vain. I will take away the hateful. Let me pass.

(She attempts to escape.)

HASSAN (*to his* SLAVES): Hold her!

(ALDER *and* WILLOW *grip each an arm.* JUNIPER *grips her ankles. She is held standing. Her cloak falls. She is clothed in short jacket and trousers of white silk with a pattern of blue flowers: her waist is naked, in the Persian style.*)

YASMIN: Ah – what will you do to me? You forgave me.

HASSAN (*to* YASMIN): Ah, I forgave you the insults and all that hour of shame. And Allah shall forgive you your trade if Allah wills. But you have pressed your foul body on mine – you have breathed your poison on my cheek, and twined your snakes (God break them!) round my breast. Prepare then to die, for it is not right for the sake of mankind that you should walk any more upon the roads of earth.

YASMIN (*quietly, but in terror*): To die! What do you mean! No, no! Ah, murder, ah!

HASSAN: Do you hear the fountain dripping – drop by drop – drop by drop? So shall your blood fall on my carpet and colour me more red flowers.

YASMIN (*recovering*): I am not afraid.

HASSAN: Do you expect mercy? I left mercy with my sweets. For all these years I have been a humble man, of soft and kindly disposition – such a man as the world and a woman hate. But now I shall never again be the fool of my fellows. Now all Bagdad shall know and say: 'We thought Hassan a mild man and a kind man; our children stole his sweets and he did but stroke his beard, while to a beggar he had known three days he would instantly lend three dinars. And behold, he has become powerful and hath cut down the body of Yasmin the infamous who had done him wrong, as a woodman cuts a tree. Yallah, our knees shall bend when Hassan goes driving by!' Yasmin, stiffen your sinews and close your eyes.

YASMIN: Not with the sword, not with the sword!

HASSAN: Let me taste the ecstasy of power. Let me drink of the fulness of life. Let me be one of those who conquer because they do not care.

(*He draws the sword:* YASMIN *cries out loud.*)

You are Yasmin, the poor, the beautiful, the proud: I am Hassan, rich and passionate and strong. You have hurt me, I will hurt you; it is the rule of the game, and the way of the world. Do I hate you? I do not know or care. Do I love you? – then love shall drive the blade in deep. You are the world's own stupendous harlot, and I will cut you clean in two.

(*He swings the sword over his head to strike.*)

YASMIN (*with a shout at once of terror and triumph*): I will not close my eyes! I will look at you. You dare not do it, looking at my eyes!

(HASSAN *whirls the sword round.*)

You dare not do it, looking at my eyes!

(HASSAN *flings the sword across the room and falls across the divan, his face in his hands.*)

HASSAN: O Hassan the Confectioner, thou art nothing but an old man and a fool!

(YASMIN *comes up to* HASSAN. *The* BOYS *silently disappear. He draws her toward him.*)

(*With infinite tenderness.*) Yasmin!

78

*The Great Hall of the Palace. The room is plain, white
marble.* ISHAK *alone, in his robes of Court Chamberlain.*
(*Enter* SOLDIERS *with the* CAPTAIN OF THE MILI-
TARY *and* CHIEF OF POLICE.)
(*The* SOLDIERS *intone 'The War Song of the Saracens.'*)
SOLDIERS *sing*:

> We are they who come faster than fate: we are they
> who ride early or late:
> We storm at your ivory gate: Pale Kings of the sunset
> beware!
> Not on silk nor in samet we lie, not in curtained solemn-
> ity die
> Among women who chatter and cry and children who
> mumble a prayer.
> But we sleep by the ropes of the camp, and we rise with
> a shout and we tramp
> With the sun or the moon for a lamp, and the spray of
> the wind in our hair.

> From the lands where the elephants are to the forts of
> Merou and Balghar,
> Our steel we have brought and our star to shine on the
> ruins of Rum.
> We have marched from the Indus to Spain, and by God
> we will go there again;
> We have stood on the shore of the plain where the
> Waters of Destiny boom.
> A mart of destruction we made at Yalula where men
> were afraid,
> For death was a difficult trade, and the sword was a
> broker of doom;

And the Spear was a Desert Physician, who cured not
a few of ambition,
And drave not a few to perdition with medicine bitter
and strong.
And the shield was a grief to the fool and as bright as a
desolate pool,
And as straight as the rock of Stamboul when their
cavalry thundered along:
For the coward was drowned with the brave when our
battle sheered up like a wave,
And the dead to the desert we gave, and the glory to
God in our song.

THE SOLDIERS (*cheering*): Allah Akbar! (*etc.*)

CHIEF OF POLICE: That is a splendid song your soldiers
sing, O breaker of infidel bones. Permit an unglorious
policeman to inquire what flaming victory you cele-
brate to-day. Such is my loathly ignorance, I knew not
the Caliph's army (may it ever plosh in seas of hostile
blood!) had even left Bagdad.

CAPTAIN OF MILITARY: It is true we have not left
Bagdad, but perchance we have saved it from destruction. For when the Caliph's Police have allowed a conspiracy to ripen undetected, it is our duty to mow down
the conspirators. It is true we did but vanquish beggars
— but they were beggars to fight. Half of them we slew
and one-half we captured, and, since the police believe
no clue but the ocular, here they are. A victory is well
worth a song.

CHIEF OF POLICE: Allah, such a song! I thought: 'At
least they have captured Cairo.'

CAPTAIN OF MILITARY: To save Bagdad is better than
to capture Cairo.

CHIEF OF POLICE (*pointing to the captive* BEGGARS):
Behold only the chain-mail of the vanquished!

CAPTAIN OF MILITARY: It is an old song, a glorious
great battle song, and in mocking it thou hast displayed
an utter absence of education, thou dragger of dead
dogs from obscure gutters.

ISHAK: Is this talk for the high divan, Captain? Ye have
saved Bagdad? Bagdad is no longer worth saving. You
rose-petal-bellied parasites of the palace, how dare you
sing that song?

CAPTAIN OF MILITARY: Allah, these Poets talk in
rhyme.

(*Enter the* HERALD *announcing various personages, who
enter as he announces them and are motioned to their place by*
ISHAK.)

HERALD: Abu Said, Prince of Basra, to do homage. Fahr-
addin, Prince of Damascus, to do homage. Al Mustan-
sir, Prince of Koniah, to do homage. Tahir Dhu'l
Yaminayn, Governor of Khorasan, to do homage.
The great caligraphist, 'Afiq of Diarbekir, master of the
riqa and the shikasta hands: also of the Peacock style,
and of painting in miniature.

ISHAK (*aside*): Episodes of considerable obscenity.

HERALD: The celebrated Turkoman wrestler, Yurghiz
Khan, whose thighs are three cubits in circumference.

ISHAK (*aside*): As fat as a woman's, but not as nice.

HERALD: Abu Nouwas, the Caliph's Jester. The Rajah of
the Upper Ganges, come hither to do homage with a
present of 800 bales of indigo.

ISHAK (*aside*): And never dyed his beard.

HERALD: Hang Wung, the wisest philosopher in China,
come hither to study the excellence of the habits of
true believers. He is a hundred and ten years old. ...

Ishak (*aside*): And perfectly blind.

Herald: Anastasius Johannes Georgius, ambassador of the infidel Empress Irene, mistress till God wills of Constantiniyeh and the lands of Rum, come here on a vain errand. ...

Ishak: He understands no word, and believes we do honour to his name. But the jest is thin, my Herald.

Herald: Abul Asal, the wandering dervish, come hither to remind kings that they are but dust.

Ishak: 'Where lies Nushiravan the Just?'

Dervish: The rhyme helps reason. In the dust.

Ishak: The platitudes of dervishes do not much disturb the beatitudes of kings.

Herald: Masrur, the Executioner, come hither to make several beggars the dusty equivalents of monarchs.

Ishak: Ah, you may well shiver, poor captives: it is draughty among your rags.

Herald: Hassan ben Hassan al Bagdadi, the Caliph's friend.

Soldiers: Long live Hassan and the shadow of Hassan and the friend of Hassan ben Hassan al Bagdadi!

Ishak (*drawing* Hassan *aside*): Come hither, friend of the Caliph; do not forget that you are the man with the broken lute.

Hassan: What is a friend?

Ishak: Are you not in favour? Has not the Caliph taught you? You have a royal friend.

Hassan: He is generous: he is gracious: he is intimate. He has leant on my arm, he has embraced me, and he has called me by that name 'friend.' But I tremble before his eyes.

Ishak: You have found out. No man can ever be his friend.

HASSAN: Alas, that is because he is exalted far above mankind!

ISHAK: Alas, no: but because he uses that supremacy to play the artist with the lives of men.

HASSAN: What do you mean, Ishak?

ISHAK: Have you not seen the designer of carpets, O Hassan of Bagdad, put here the blue and here the gold, here the orange and here the green? So have I seen the Caliph take the life of some helpless man – who was contented in his little house and garden, enjoying the blue of happy days – and colour his life with the purple of power, and streak it with the crimson of lust: then whelm it all in the gloom-greys of abasement, touched with the glaring reds of pain, and edge the whole with the black border of annihilation.

HASSAN: He has been so generous. Do not say he is a tyrant! Do not say he delights in the agony of men!

ISHAK: Agony is a fine colour, and he delights therein as a painter in vermilion new brought from Kurdistan. But shall so great an artist not love contrast? To clasp a silver belt round the loins of a filthy beggar while a slave darkens the soles of his late vizier, is for him but a jest touched with a sense of the appropriate: and I have seen it enacted in this very room.

HASSAN: But you are his friend.

ISHAK: As you are. It is elegant for a monarch to condescend: it is refreshing for a monarch to talk as man to man. It is artistic for a monarch to enjoy the pleasures of contrast and escape the formalities of Court. ... But here comes the preceder of the Caliph, the penultimate splendour of the divan, a man noble without passion, sagacious without inspiration, and weak as a miser's coffee.

HERALD: The Tulip of the Parterre of Government, the Shadow of the Cypress Tree, the Sun's Moon, Jafar the Barmecide.

SOLDIERS: Long live the great Vizier!

HERALD: Let all mouths close but mine. (*Lifting his staff.*) The Holy, the Just, the High-born, the Omnipotent; the Gardener of the Vale of Islam, the Lion of the Imperial Forests, the Rider on the Spotless Horse, the Cypress on the Golden Hill, the Master of Spears, the Redresser of Wrong, the Drinker of Blood, the Peacock of the World, the Shadow of God on Earth, the Commander of the Faithful, Haroun ar Raschid ben Mohammed, Ibn Abdullah Ibn Mohammed Ibn Ali ben Abdullah, Ibn 'Abbas, the Caliph!

SOLDIERS: The Holy, the High-born, the Just One, the Caliph!

The Cypress, the Peacock, the Lion, the Caliph!

From Rum to Bokhara one monarch, the Caliph!

DERVISH (*gloomily*): A clay thing, a plaything, a shadow, the Caliph!

CALIPH: The Divan is open. Let all mouths close but mine. Our justice to-day will be swift as a blow of the sword. In the Book of the Wisdom of Rulers I read: 'Be sudden to uproot the tree of conspiracy for it scatters far its seed.' Are you the Beggars?

BEGGARS: We are beggars of Bagdad.

CALIPH: Thou, spokesman, come hither! Wherefore didst thou plot against my throne and the safety of all Islam? Didst thou not fear not only for thy life but for thy salvation?

BEGGAR: Master and Lord of the World, hast thou been poor, hast thou been hungry? Dost thou know what dreams enter the gaunt heads of starving men as they lie against the back of thy garden wall, and moan: 'Bread in God's name, bread in the name of God?'

CALIPH: Dost thou deny conspiracy?

BEGGAR: I conspired.

CALIPH: Is there one of you denieth conspiracy?

(*Silence.*)

Masrur, lead out the conspirators to death.

(MASRUR *executes the order.*)

CALIPH: Let those whose duty it is fetch him who is called the King of the Beggars from his cell, and let him who did us the great service of capturing alive that dangerous man, step forth into the midst.

CHIEF OF POLICE (*stepping forward*): Lord of the World – but I am dirt.

CAPTAIN OF MILITARY (*simultaneously advancing*): Lord of the World – but I am dung.

CALIPH: Were you both concerned in his capture? My favour is doubled upon you. Let two robes of honour be brought before my throne.

CHIEF OF POLICE: Sir, I fail to comprehend the presence of this military man. He was but a spectator when I dragged out the King of the Beggars from the gutter of his roof.

CAPTAIN OF MILITARY: O thou civilian, I caught a valiant hold of his legs, despite his heavy and continuous kicks, whilst thou didst but timidly pluck at his sleeve.

CHIEF OF POLICE: Pluck at his sleeve, thou tin-coated murderer! Summon the twenty drops of blood that trickle round thy lank and withered frame and let them mount to thy mendacious cheek!

CAPTAIN OF MILITARY: Thou dropsical elephant!

CALIPH: Enough! I love to hear the speech of heroes, but

enough. It is clear the glory is divided. Give me one of those robes of honour, and summon the tailor of the court.

COURT TAILOR (*very prostrate*): O Master of the World, O Master!

CALIPH: Slit me this robe in twain.

COURT TAILOR (*moaning as he does so*): Allah is great, Allah is great. Such a well-cut robe: such excellent silk!

CALIPH: Come hither both.

CAPTAIN OF MILITARY (*hanging back*): The glory is all to the Police.

CHIEF OF POLICE: The credit is entirely due to my honourable friend.

CALIPH (*insisting*): Come hither both.

(*They are fitted with half a robe of honour each amid laughter.*)

SOLDIERS: Long live those whom the Caliph delights to honour!

CAPTAIN OF MILITARY (*under his teeth*): Mutinous swine.

CALIPH: And now bring forward the King of the Beggars.

(*The KING OF THE BEGGARS is brought in chained hand and foot, but still dressed in gold.*)

The Salaam to my host of yesternight.

RAFI, KING OF BEGGARS: The Salaam, O man of Basra. I see thy fellow-merchant in the robes of the Grand Vizier. But the negro, that most disgusting negro, seems to be absent. To Hassan, my congratulations on his advancement.

CALIPH: Thou dost speak with the impudence of a king, but thy subjects are taken from thee. They will soon be black crows in the pine-wood by the walls.

RAFI: Had I but known thee last night, thou man of

Basra, whom men call Caliph of the Faithful – O thou massacrer of good men – had I but known thee, had I but known thee!

CHIEF OF POLICE: Shall I tear out his tongue?

CALIPH: Let him talk. I have found a man who does not flatter me. Let me study the hatred in his eyes.

RAFI: It is not enough for thee to misrule a quarter of the world. Thou art not only a fool tyrant, but a mean tradesman, thou dog-hearted spy!.

JAFAR: It is not decent to let this man continue his coarse abuse, O Master. Wilt thou not end him?

CALIPH: He shall end in his time. (*To* KING OF THE BEGGARS.) Thy impudence will not redound to thy advantage, Rafi! Wherefore dost thou not bite the tongue of insolence with the tooth of discretion?

RAFI: I am a man in the presence of death.

CALIPH: There are a thousand paths to the delectable tavern of death, and some run straight and some run crooked.

RAFI: Cut, scourge, burn, rack thy utmost. The nobler the aim the baser the failure. Do not I deserve to feel every separate pain of those whom my folly has sent to a cruel death?

CHINESE PHILOSOPHER: I am a hundred and ten years old, and I have never heard a remark in more exquisite taste.

CALIPH: It is well. But before I send thee to a death so cruel that thy conscience shall be fully satisfied in this world and the next, answer me this: Hast thou forgotten that unparalleled lady whom the zeal of my servants ravished from thy embrace?

RAFI: Thou devil of Eblis! Have I forgotten? Have I not prayed thou shouldst forget?

CALIPH: Shall a gallant man forget the name of a beautiful woman? We will look on her, for whom thou didst attempt to raze the central fort of Islam. (*To* ATTENDANTS.) Bring in this lady, Pervaneh.

RAFI (*in supplication*): O Master of the World! O Master of the World!

CALIPH: Thou changest tone abruptly but late.

RAFI: I was insolent only that her name should be forgotten in thy anger and my death, O Splendour of Islam!

CALIPH: A crafty excuse for impoliteness. Wilt thou now begin to be polite to the tyrant whose coffin was to be nailed over his open eyes? He who hopes for his audience to forget the subject of his discourse should moderate his style.

RAFI: God blind me that I may not see her!

CALIPH: Why? Dost thou not love her still? Is not the sight of his beloved to the victim of separation like the vision of a fountain to him who dies of thirst?

HASSAN (*aside*): But if that fountain be a fountain whose drops are blood?

RAFI: Thou, thou hast held her in thy arms! O God, have pity on my soul!

CALIPH: But with this knowledge thou didst still desire her, and wast ready to wreck Bagdad for the sparkle of her eyes.

RAFI: But first the blood of her possessor should have washed her honour clean.

CALIPH: Thou art a most ridiculous man. Thou hast built thy monstrous tower of crime on a foundation of painted smoke. Dost thou imagine I have tasted all the fruit of my garden?

RAFI: Allah has given thee men's bodies, but it is for him

alone to torment the soul. By thy faith, O Caliph, speak the truth!

CALIPH: Do I know every slave whom my industrious officials sweep in from the streets? To my knowledge I have never set my eyes on this woman of thine.

HERALD: The maiden Pervaneh!

CALIPH: Let her come before me.

(PERVANEH *is ushered into the Presence.*)

PERVANEH (*with due reverence*): O Master of the World!

CALIPH: It is written in the Sacred Law: In the King's presence a woman may unveil, without fear of censure.

PERVANEH: Ah, Master, but only the eagle dare look upon the sun.

CALIPH: Thy speech is proud enough for all the eagles, Lady Pervaneh, and I doubt not thy eyes, which I desire to see, are steady in the blaze of danger. Must I command thee to unveil?

PERVANEH: Alas, Master of the World, my eyes are dim with long confinement in a jewelled cage, and the wings of my soul are numb. Only on the hills of my country where the rolling sun of Heaven has his morning home, only on their windy hills do the women of my country go unveiled.

ISHAK (*to himself, half singing*): The hills, the hills, the morning on the hills!

CALIPH (*to* PERVANEH): I command thee to unveil.

PERVANEH: If thou wilt tear my veil off my face, I will tear my face before thy eyes.

RAFI: Ah, no! ...

PERVANEH: Who art thou who dost cry, 'Ah, no!'? Who art thou who dost hide thy face in fettered hands ...

RAFI: A prisoner.

PERVANEH: dissembling thy voice ...

89

RAFI: A prisoner awaiting death.

PERVANEH: trembling when I touch thee?

RAFI: A man afraid.

PERVANEH (*in a voice of exaltation*): For thee, Sultan, I raise my veil; and wait thy captive, to share thy destiny.

HASSAN: Oh, Ishak! The fire of the heart of beauty!

RAFI: Leave me, Pervaneh! Walk not upon my path! You do not know what a foul doom is mine.

PERVANEH: Foul dooms? Foul dooms? Rafi, I can forget ten centuries of doom now that I see your eyes again!

RAFI: I conspired against his throne to win you freedom. Through my fault I failed, through my fault my thousand followers are dancing in the wind.

PERVANEH: For me you conspired? For me – for me?

RAFI: I would have drowned Bagdad in blood to kiss your lips again.

PERVANEH: O lover!

RAFI (*showing his fettered hands*): Lover indeed!

PERVANEH: There are a thousand eyes round us, O my beloved, but what care I? The voice of the world cries out, 'Thou art a slave in the Palace, and thy lover a prisoner in chains.' (*Embracing him.*) But we have heard the Trumpets of Reality that drown the vain din of the Thing that Seems. We have walked with the Friend of Friends in the Garden of the Stars, and He is pitiable to poor lovers who are pierced by the arrows of this ghostly world. Your lips are the only lips, my lover, your eyes the only eyes – and all the other eyes but phantom lights that glitter in the mist of dream.

COURTIER: This is sheer heresy.

ISHAK: Then a plague on your religion.

JAFAR: This is Sufic doctrine, and most dangerous to the State.

HASSAN: Then a plague on the state!

CALIPH: Ye who make love in full Divan, can ye yet listen to the voice of the world?

PERVANEH (*dazed*): They are speaking.

CALIPH: O Rafi, King of the Beggars, since after all thou art much entangled in the web of unreality, it is necessary that I ask thee some phantom questions concerning thy apparent acts.

Firstly, dost thou deny thou didst call thyself Caliph of the Unbelievers, and blaspheme thy faith in my presence and in the presence of Jafar, my Vizier, Masrur, the Executioner, and Hassan, my friend?

RAFI: I have nothing to deny.

CALIPH: Dost thou, secondly, deny that thou didst swear in the presence of the same to nail the Caliph of the Faithful alive in his coffin, or that thou didst conspire with the beggars to slay me, to seize Bagdad and to usurp the throne?

RAFI: I have nothing to deny.

CALIPH: Dost thou, thirdly, deny that thou didst scheme this monstrous crime for the sake of a woman?

RAFI: I have nothing to deny.

CALIPH: Rafi, thou art confessed a Blasphemer, a Traitor ... and a Lunatic. It remains to consider thy punishment.

RAFI: As thou wilt.

CALIPH: Thou art brave, but I fear the shafts of unreality will prick thee extremely hard. For thou hast merited not one but a dozen deaths. Now, if I impale thee for conspiracy, how shall I burn thee for blasphemy? But with such other pains as man can suffer, judicious arrangement carries the day over unthinking brutality. For if I skin thee for thy impudence, how can I flog thee for thy folly? But if the order is reversed thou canst enjoy the benefit of both expiations.

RAFI: Thou hast certainly studied the art of pain.

CALIPH: Yet what are the worst tortures thou shalt undergo to the horror of the death thou didst contrive for me?

RAFI (*with impatience*): What is my condemnation?

CALIPH: For Lunacy to be nailed, for Conspiracy to be stretched, for Blasphemy to be split.

PERVANEH: Ah!

(*Murmurs of horror and satisfaction fill the Court at the announcement of this savage punishment.*)

RAFI: As Allah wills.

PERVANEH (*falling at the* CALIPH's *feet*): Spare, spare, O Master of the World!

CALIPH: Dost thou think I will absolve him for thy 'spare'?

PERVANEH: Mercy! Oh, Mercy!

CALIPH: Why dost thou cry 'Mercy' and clasp my feet? Is not pain a fancy and this world a cloud?

PERVANEH (*rising to her feet*): This world is Hell, but those that dig Hell deeper shall find the Hell-beneath-the-Hells which they search for.

CALIPH: Thou hast metaphysic, but hast thou logic? Invent me a reason – one small and subtle reason – why I should show mercy to this man.

PERVANEH: Ah – wilt thou have reasons?

CALIPH: Was not my sentence just?

PERVANEH: Wilt thou have justice?

CALIPH: If I had stood bound before him, would he have listened to my prayer?

PERVANEH: Wilt thou have revenge?

CALIPH: Shall I scorn reason, pervert justice, and put aside revenge – for thy dark eyes?

PERVANEH: Turn thy justice, turn thy revenge on me in the name of the dark eyes of God! They say a woman suffers longer and sharper than a man.

CALIPH: Lady, dost thou mean this with all its meaning, or say it to implore pity? Beware of thy answer! The rack and whip are ready and near at hand.

PERVANEH (*her arms outstretched*): Then give the word. Knock off those fetters before my eyes – and nail me to the wall.

RAFI: Pervaneh!

CALIPH: Ecstasy! Ecstasy! Thou art an ecstatic and wilt not suffer. I know the thick skins of martyrs. I refuse.

PERVANEH (*to* RAFI): Alas, what can I do!

RAFI: Let me die! I have seen you again. It is nothing for a man to die.

PERVANEH: Nothing for a man to die? 'Tis Heaven wide open for a man to die. But they will tear you, Rafi, Rafi!

RAFI: Shall I fear the pain you called upon yourself, or shrink where you were brave?

PERVANEH (*to the* CALIPH): I ask so small a boon. Grant my lover a clean death!

CALIPH: Thou dost ask a very great boon indeed. For as thou sayest, what is death? Shall the man who shakes my kingdom slip into eternity like a thief men catch in the bazaar? Shall he who does the greater wrong not suffer the greater pain?

PERVANEH: He is not afraid of pain.

CALIPH: That is not to say he feels not pain.

PERVANEH: Just and reasonable, yet there is a holier thing than reason and justice.

DERVISH (*his orthodoxy disturbed*): A holier thing than justice?

93

PERVANEH: Yes, Dervish. There is that which should not be defiled.

CALIPH: Whither now does thy plea wander?

PERVANEH: O Father of Islam, can thine eyes that love flowers behold man's body hewn into foul shapes and monstrous as the phantoms that go wailing round the graves? Can thy ears that love the music of Ishak, listen to the gasps of the tormented·droning through their bodies like a winter wind among the pines?

CALIPH: I shall not honour Rafi with my attendance: I shall be far from sight and sound.

PERVANEH: The thought of it – the thought of it!

CALIPH: I have been ordering executioners all my life. There is only one thought that can haunt me – the thought of a coffin closing on open eyes, the sway of the coffin carried to the grave, the crash at the bottom of the pit, the rumble of the earth on the lid, the gasping for breath and light.

PERVANEH: He was distraught by passion, he spoke in fury: but thou dost judge him with a quiet mind. He is a man among men, but thou art the representative of God on earth, the sole Priest of Islam. Thou shalt not order God's image to be defiled.

CALIPH: So you would have me spare him for the sake of the perfection of man's body? O Pervaneh, I am far more likely to spare him for the perfection of woman's.

PERVANEH (*shrinking from the implied menace*): For those that have wits, O Master, perfection is sundered from desire.

CALIPH: You are a woman – perfect – but a woman.

PERVANEH: By the curse of God.

CALIPH: And however much you sunder perfection from desire, from desire your perfection is not sundered.

94

PERVANEH: I am the slave of thy household to come or go, to fetch or carry, to be struck or slain: but my perfection is not the slave of thy desire.

CALIPH (*softly*): Yet, if you return to my household ...

PERVANEH (*in fury*): To die.

CALIPH: You would not be forgotten or neglected ... and your presence would be a consolation and a charm ...

PERVANEH: Not to you, frigid tyrant, not to you!

CALIPH (*softly*): Nor yet to the man who let your lover go in peace?

PERVANEH: Is there no shame in the world of Islam? Will you unclothe your lust in full Divan!

CALIPH: You have already given the example. Come, shall I set your lover free?

PERVANEH: I would choke if you touched me, I would choke. Oh, the shame on me, the shame! You are smiling. It is not me you want but my shame! Is there a God in heaven that lets you sit and smile! But you can set him free. Ah, will you set him free? I am your slave — I am your slave. You can rob me of rope and knife — the very means of death. If you will set him free! I am your slave, what choice have I?

CALIPH: Thou hast not the manners or the heart of a slave. Thou wast brought to my household by violence, a free woman born, and art no slave of mine. In the presence of my Divan I pronounce thee free. Thou art free to come and free to go, free to buy and free to sell, free to walk out and free to stay, free to wed and free to die — and free to make a choice ...

PERVANEH: To make a choice? What choice? Between his death and my dishonour?

CALIPH: No, between love and life.

PERVANEH: Explain, O Master of the World!

CALIPH: Between two deaths with torment and two lives with separation. Between a day of love and all the years of life.

PERVANEH: Enlighten my understanding.

CALIPH: I have considered this matter, I have decided this matter. I will speak plain and clear. (*Rising.*) This is my irrevocable judgment from which there is no appeal. I give a choice to Pervaneh and Rafi, the King of the Beggars, and I grant them till sunset to consult their hearts and make that choice together. They shall both live on these conditions: that the lady Pervaneh return forthwith to my harem to be my wife in lawful wedlock, and be treated with all the honour her boldness and her beauty merit. That the King of the Beggars leave Bagdad, and that these two lovers part for ever till they die.

But if they refuse this separation, I offer them one day of love, from sunset to-night to sunset on the morrow, unfettered and alone, with no more guard than may keep them from self-destruction. But when that day is over they shall die together in merciless torment. In the name of Allah the most merciful, the Divan is closed.

CURTAIN

ACT IV

SCENE I

In the vaults of the palace, outside the cell of the KING OF
THE BEGGARS. *Drop Scene.*

(*Enter* HASSAN.)

HASSAN: Which way? Which way? I am lost in this dark
passage. My voice rings round the arches. What's that
noise? Is there an army coming? Or are all the prisoners
stamping with wrath? ... No ... It is only someone walking. ... I wonder who! And if this stranger asks me my
business what shall I say to him? Do I know what
brought me to this dismal region?

ISHAK (*from the darkness*): Who goes there? What dost
thou here? What is thy business?

HASSAN: Who calls? I am Hassan, inspecting the security
of the imperial prisons. Who art thou?

ISHAK: Who am I? Ten books were written by Aflatun
and twenty by Aristu to answer that mighty question,
O Hassan of my heart!

HASSAN: Ishak! Come out of hiding, Ishak. What are you
doing here?

ISHAK: I gather mushrooms, O inspector of the vaults of
vice!

HASSAN: Have you come too? I do not know why I came.
I hoped ... I do not know why I came, but I think our
hearts do beat together like the hearts of friends. Did
you come here because of *them?*

ISHAK: I came here to hear a play more tragic than the

mysteries of Hossein, to listen to a debate more weighty than the council talk of kings. ...

HASSAN: You do not mean? ...

ISHAK: I mean the debate of love and life.

HASSAN: Could you spy on that? How cruel!

ISHAK: The poet must learn what man's agony can teach him.

HASSAN: Is it then not better not to be a poet?

ISHAK (*bitterly*): Allah did not ask me that question when he made me a poet and a dissector of souls. It is my trade: I do but follow my master, the exalted Designer of human carpets, the Ruler of the world. If he prepared the situation, shall I not observe the characters? Thus I corrupt my soul to create – Allah knoweth what – ten little words like rubies glimmering in a row. As for you, I think you begin to understand the Caliph of the Faithful.

HASSAN: Why speak of him? All men are brutes, you and he and I. I thought that I was kinder than other men – but I was only more afraid. This day is the first day of my exaltation, I have begun it the all but murderer of a woman, and I end it a spy on souls in trouble.

ISHAK: Do not worry any longer, dear Hassan, on the moral problem. The moth of curiosity will always flutter round the lamp of circumstance. Here comes the guard, they shall direct us.

(*Enter* 2 GUARDS.)

ISHAK (*to the* GUARD): Ho, soldier, whither?

1ST GUARD (*saluting*): To the cell of the King of the Beggars, my masters, to relieve the Guard.

ISHAK: What, will you stand inside the cell?

1ST GUARD: Inside, O my masters.

ISHAK: A shame, I say, a shame to spy on a pair of lovers.

Will they fly off through the grating or creep through the keyhole?

1ST GUARD: We know the ways of prisoners, O my masters. Masrur is disappointed when we bring him corpses to be whipped. (*To* 2ND GUARD.) Is he not disappointed, Mohamed?

2ND GUARD (*in deep, lugubrious and respectful tones*): Oh, sir, he is bitterly disappointed.

ISHAK: Well, it is your fault, my fine fellows, if you leave daggers and ropes lying about in your prisoners' cells?

1ST GUARD: Ah, you do not know the artfulness of prisoners, my masters. They will bang their heads against the wall, or they will eat their straw. (*To* 2ND GUARD.) Do they not eat their straw, Mohamed?

2ND GUARD (*to* ISHAK): Oh, sir, they frequently eat their straw.

ISHAK: Chain them, chain them.

1ST GUARD: We do, my masters, but even then they strangle themselves in their fetters.

ISHAK: Strangle themselves in their fetters?

1ST GUARD: Do they not strangle themselves in their fetters, Mohamed?

2ND GUARD (*to* ISHAK): I have known them, sir, to strangle themselves in their fetters.

ISHAK: But, as you know, these two have a choice between a life with separation and a death with torment. Now surely they will choose life, and will hardly need a sentry to spear them away from the doorstep of eternity.

1ST GUARD: I should think so indeed, sir. But you never can tell with prisoners. Prisoners are very obstinate, especially women, are they not, Mohamed?

2ND GUARD (*to* ISHAK): Female prisoners are very obstinate indeed, sir.

ISHAK (*with assumed heartiness*): Well, none of us would require till sunset to make our choice, would we?

1ST GUARD. No, sir, not those of us who have ever seen Masrur at work.

ISHAK: But if they do choose their day of love, will they not be free according to the Caliph's promise? Will you still guard them in their cell, O sons of impropriety, lest they eat their straw?

1ST GUARD (*with a leer*): Nay, we shall stand outside the door, and listen at the grill.

ISHAK: And that is precisely what we intend to do now if you will show us the door.

1ST GUARD: I don't know whether I could quite do that, sir.

ISHAK (*giving him money*): You are valiant fellows and, I am convinced, considerably underpaid.

1ST GUARD: Ours is a most disagreeable profession, your Excellency.

2ND GUARD (*accepting money*): And the emoluments are infinitesimal.

1ST GUARD: This way, gentlemen.

(*Shows them to the door.*)

SCENE II

A cell. A grating through which streams the sunlight. A heavy door with a narrow spyhole. RAFI *is fettered to the wall, but* PERVANEH *has not been bound.* TWO GUARDS *stand immobile on either side of the door.*

RAFI: They have changed our guard for the last time; it will be sunset in an hour.

PERVANEH: Still a long hour before your hands are freed to make me a belt of love. Oh, idle sun, I am

100

weary of thy pattern on the wall. Still a long hour!

RAFI: And still a night and a day before our doom.

PERVANEH: Why is your voice so sorrowful? Your words do not keep step with your decision nor march like standard-bearers of your great resolve.

RAFI: What have I decided? What have I resolved? You came near. I saw the wings of your spirit beating the air around you. You locked the silver fetters around my neck and I forgot these manacles of iron: you perfumed me with your hair till this cell became a meadow: you turned toward me eyes in whose night the seven deep oceans flashed their drowned stars, and all your body asked without speech, 'Wilt thou die for love?'

PERVANEH: Do you repent? Do you unsay the golden words?

RAFI: Put but your lips on mine and seal my words against unsaying!

PERVANEH: I did wrong to make you passionate. I see that in your heart you do repent. I would not have you bound by a moment's madness but wish all your reason and with all your soul.

RAFI: Ah, stand apart and veil your face, you who call in the name of reason! You are all afire for martyrdom: can you hear reason calling from her snows? Oh, you woman, Allah curse you for blinding my eyes with love!

PERVANEH: Ah, Rafi!

RAFI: Be silent — be silent! Your voice is the voice of a garden at daybreak, when all the birds are singing at the sun. Forget your whirling dreams, your fires, your lightnings, your splendours of the soul, and answer the passionless voice that asks you — why should your lover die, and such a death?

PERVANEH: I am listening.

RAFI: I am very young. Shall I forget to laugh if I continue to live? Shall I spend all my hours regretting you? Shall I not return to my country and comfort the hearts of those that gave me birth? Have I not my white-walled house, my books, my old friends, my garden of flowers and trees? Has the stream forgotten to sing at the end of my garden because Pervaneh comes no more? 'Love fades,' saith Reason, with a gentler voice. 'Love fades, but doth not fall. Love fadeth not to yellow like the rose but to gold like the leaves upon the poplar by the stream.' And when my poplars are all gold, I shall sit beneath their shade beside the stream to read my book. When I am tired of my book I will lie on my back and watch the clouds. There in the clouds I shall see your face, and remember you with a wistful remembrance as if you had always been a dream and the silver torment of your arms had never been more than the white mists circling the round mountain snows.

PERVANEH (*with growing anger*): And so, wrapped in pleasant fancies, you will forget the woman whose honour you have sold to a tyrant. And so, while I, far from my country and my home, am dying of shame and confinement, you will dream and you will dream!

RAFI: The plague on your dishonour! You are to be the Caliph's wife. Is that not held in all Islam for the highest honour to which a woman can attain? Is that worse shame than being flayed by a foul negro? The shame! the selling! the dishonour! A woman's vanity: am I to be tortured to death to gratify your pride? If I must not have you, do I care whose wife you be? I shall remember you as you are now — rock water undefiled.

PERVANEH: Cold and heartless coward: you are afraid of death!

RAFI: By Allah, I am afraid of death, and the man who fears not death is a dullard and a fool! Are we still making speeches in full Divan to the admiration of the bystanders? Must we pose even now! If you hate me for fearing death, go your way and leave this coward. Ah, no, no, do not leave me, O Pervaneh! Forgive me that I am what I am. I have not unsaid my promise. I will die with you. I will die! I will die! I will endure the tortures that are thrice as terrible as death, the tortures that parch my mouth with fear.

PERVANEH: Shame on you, weak and shivering lover! What is pain for us!

RAFI: You do not see — you do not see! Look at your hands, they shall be torn — ah, I cannot speak of it. I shall see your blood flow like wine from a white fountain drop by drop till you have painted the carpet of execution all red lilies.

PERVANEH: Ah — but will not even your poor love flow deep when I set that crimson seal upon the story of our lives!

RAFI: Alas, you are still dreaming: you are still blind with exaltation: your speech is metaphor. You do not see, you have never heard the high, thin shriek of the tortured, you have not seen the shape of their bodies when they are cast into the ditch. Come near, Pervaneh. Do you know what they will do to you? Come near: I cannot say it aloud. (PERVANEH *approaches*.) Ah, I dare not tell you. ... I dare not tell you!

PERVANEH: Tell me, clear and plain.

RAFI (*whispers in* PERVANEH'S *ear*): ...

PERVANEH (*covering her face with her hands*): Ah, God — they will do that! No, no; they will not do that to me!

RAFI: Pitilessly.

PERVANEH (*wildly*): They will do that! – Ah, the shame of it! They will do that – Ah, the pain of it! I see! I feel! I hear! O save me, Rafi!

RAFI: Alas! Why did I tell you this?

PERVANEH: It is beyond endurance: it is foul: my veins will burst at the very thought. I am between a shame and a shame and there is no escape. ... But, at least, they shall not do this to you, Rafi. Hush ... talk low: the soldiers must not hear. (*Glancing at the* GUARDS *and whispering low.*) Will you die here between my hands, instantly, and with no pain?

RAFI (*in a hushed voice*): Quickly! How can you do it? We are guarded – have you a knife?

PERVANEH: My hands will be cunning round your neck, beloved. Did I not say you should die between my hands?

RAFI: Be quick: be quiet: I will cast back my head.

A GUARD (*thrusting* PERVANEH *back with his drawn sword as she lays her hands on her lover's neck*): Back, in the Caliph's name!

RAFI (*to* PERVANEH): Run in upon his sword. ...

PERVANEH (*shrinking away from the* GUARD'S *sword*): I cannot!

RAFI: Quick – quick! Fall on the sword and save all shame.

PERVANEH: My breast, my breast: I am afraid .. (*Prostrate on the ground.*) I am utterly shamed – I have missed your death and mine.

RAFI: You have flinched.

PERVANEH: The point was on my breast, and it might have been all ended for you and me.

RAFI: You have been afraid.

PERVANEH: It would have driven to my heart. Ah, the woman that I am!

RAFI: It is so small a thing, a pricking of the steel.

PERVANEH: Ah! – it is a little thing, you say? It is like ice, so sharp and cold. I am a vile coward.

RAFI: We are both cowards, you and I. The sunlight changes on the wall from white to gold. It is evening. Our time has come. Shall we choose life? Shall we choose the sky and the sea, the mountains, the rivers and the plains? Shall we choose the flowers and the bees, and all the birds of heaven? Shall we choose laughter and tears, sorrow and desire, speech and silence, and the shout of the man behind the hill?

PERVANEH: Ah, empty, empty without your heart! (*Weeps.*)

RAFI: Empty as death, Pervaneh, empty as death?

PERVANEH: The wall reddens: the last minute has come: we must choose.

RAFI: Choose for me: I follow. Did I talk of life? My heart is breaking for desire of you. If you bid me depart, I will not live without you. Choose for me – and choose well. Phantoms of pain! Phantoms of pain! Let me but have you in my arms, and one day of love shall widen into eternity. Who knows? The earth may crack to-night, or the sun stay down for ever in his grave. Who knows – to-morrow – God will begin, and finish the judgment of the world – and when it is all over find you sleeping in my arms?

PERVANEH (*rising slowly to her feet and laying her hands on the shoulders of her lover*): Oh, let us die! Not for my dishonour, Rafi. What is my dishonour to me or you, beloved, or the shame of a girl's virginity to him who made the sea? This clay of mine is fair enough, I think, but God hath cast it in the common mould. O lover, lover, I would walk beneath the walls and sell my body to the gipsy and the Jew ere you should cry 'I am hungry' or 'I am cold.'

RAFI: Die for love of me — for a day and a night of love!

PERVANEH: I die for love of you, Rafi! Behold, the Spirit grows bright around you: you are one with the Eternal Lover, the Friend of all the World. His spirit flashes in thine eyes and hovers round thy lips: thy body is all fire!

RAFI: Comfort me, comfort me! I do not understand thy dreams.

PERVANEH (*her arms stiffening in ecstasy*): The splendour pours from the window — the spirits in red and gold. Death with thee, death for thee, death to attain thee, O lover — and then the garden — then the fountain — then the walking side by side.

RAFI: O my sweet life, O my sweet life — must this mad dreaming end thee?

PERVANEH: Sweet life — we die for thy sweetness, O Lord of the Garden of Peace! Come, love, for the fire that beats within us, for the air that blows around us, for the mountains of our country and the wind among their pines and I accept torture and confront our end. We are in the service of the World. The voice of the rolling deep is shouting: 'Suffer that my waves may moan.' The company of the stars sing out: 'Be brave that we may shine.' The spirits of children not yet born whisper as they crowd around us: 'Endure that we may conquer.'

RAFI: Pervaneh! Pervaneh!

PERVANEH: Hark! Hark! — down through the spheres — the Trumpeter of Immortality! 'Die, lest I be shamed, lovers. Die, lest I be shamed!'

RAFI: Die then, Pervaneh, for thy great reasons. Me no ecstasy can help through the hours of pain. I die for love alone.

HERALD (*entering*): The Caliph demands your choice.
RAFI: Death!
HASSAN (*bursting in*): No, no. O God!
ISHAK: They have chosen too well.
(*Exit* HERALD. PERVANEH *is still in ecstasy when the curtain falls.*)

END OF ACT IV

ACT V

SCENE I

Towards the sunset of the next day. The CALIPH'S *garden* (ACT III, SCENE I) *once more.*
(*Enter the* CALIPH *with* ATTENDANTS *as* HASSAN *comes from his pavilion.*)

CALIPH: We were coming to your door to seek you, Hassan, but you have anticipated the knock of doubt by the shock of appearance. Why have you left your house before the nightingale? Will you too sing to the dawning moon? If so — we have come to hear.

HASSAN: Oh, Master of the World — the hour of the nightingale has not yet come. I have sought thee all day, O Master, and could not find thee. Thou didst hold the Divan — thou wast hunting — thou wast asleep — thou wast at dinner — and now the hour is near, O Master of the World — but not yet come.

CALIPH: What hour?

HASSAN: The hour of the nightingale: the hour when sun and moon are weighed in the silver scales of heaven: and thy scale of justice moves downward with the sun.

CALIPH: Surely thy head is full of fancies and thy mood perverse. I cannot grasp the shadow of thy meaning.

HASSAN (*throwing himself at the* CALIPH'S *feet*): O Master of the World, have mercy on Pervaneh and Rafi!

CALIPH: What — those two? Let them have mercy on themselves. They have chosen death as I am told. The woman has paid me the compliment of preferring torture with her Rafi to a marriage with myself. They have spent a pleasant day together: exquisite food was placed before them, and the surveillance was discreet. They will now pass a less pleasant evening.

HASSAN: Let not the woman be tortured: have mercy on the woman!

CALIPH: Rise, you fantastic suppliant. Do you dare ask mercy for these insolent and dangerous folk whose life was in their own hands – who have themselves pulled down the cord of the rat-trap of destruction?

HASSAN: Had you but heard them – had you but watched as I did while they made that awful choice, you would have forgotten expediency, justice, revenge, and listened only to the appeal of the anguish of their souls!

CALIPH: I doubt it!

HASSAN: They chose so well! They are so young. So terribly in love. I have not slept, I have not eaten, Master! I take no pleasure in my house and garden. I see blood on my walls, blood on my carpet, blood in the fountain, blood in the sky!

CALIPH: Well, well, I will leave you to these agreeable delusions. Abu Nawas has found me a young Kurdish girl who can dance with one leg round her neck, and knows by heart the song of Alexander. I perceive you will be no fit companion for an evening's sport.

HASSAN: It is only for the torture that I speak: it is only for the woman that I implore. Say but one word: the sun will set so soon.

CALIPH (angrily): If thou and Ishak, and Jafar and the Governors of all the provinces were prostrate with supplication before me, I would not spare her one caress of Masrur's black hand.

HASSAN (*springing to his feet and making at the* CALIPH):
   Hideous tyrant, torturer from Hell!

CALIPH (*coolly, as* GUARDS *seize* HASSAN): You surprise
   me. Since when have confectioners become so tigerish
   in their deportment?

HASSAN (*terrified*): What have I said! What have I done!

CALIPH: There speaks the old confectioner again.

HASSAN: I am not ashamed to be a confectioner, but I am
   ashamed to be a coward.

CALIPH: Do not despair, good Hassan. You would not
   take my warning: you have left the Garden of Art for
   the Palace of Action: you have troubled your head with
   the tyranny of princes, and the wind of complication is
   blowing through your shirt. You will forfeit your house
   and be banished from the Garden, for you are not fit to
   be the friend of kings. But for the rest, since you did me
   great service the other night, go in peace, and all the
   confectionery of the Palace shall be ordered at your
   shop.

HASSAN: Master, for this mercy I thank you humbly.

CALIPH: For nothing – for nothing! I make allowance for
   the purple thread of madness woven in the camel-cloth
   of your character. I know your head is affected by a
   caloric afternoon. Indeed, I sympathise with the interest
   you have shown as to the fate of Pervaneh and Rafi, and
   as a mark of favour I offer you a place among the spec-
   tators of their execution.

HASSAN: Ah, no, no! – that I could never bear to see!

CALIPH: Moreover, as a special token of my esteem, I will
   not send you to the execution – I will bring the execution here, and have it held in your honour. You dreamt
   that your walls were sweating blood. I will fulfil the
   prophecy implied and make the dream come true.

HASSAN: I shall never sleep again!

CALIPH (*to* ATTENDANT): Take my ring; go to the postern gate, intercept the procession of Protracted Death, and bid Masrur bring his prisoners to this pavilion and slay them on the carpet he shall find within the walls.

HASSAN: Master! Master! Is it not enough? I must go back to my trade and the filth of the Bazaar: I must be a poor man again and the fool of poor men. 'Look at Hassan,' men will say, 'he has had his day of greatness: look at that greasy person: he has been clothed in gold: let us therefore go and insult the man who was once the Caliph's friend: let us draw moral lessons from him on the mutability of human affairs.' But I, disregarding their jeers and insolent compassion, wrapping my body in my cloak and my soul in contemplation, would have remembered my day of pride, this Garden of Great Peace, this Fountain of Charm, this Pavilion of Beatitude: I would have recollected that I once had talked with Poets of the art of poetry, and owned slaves as pretty as their names. Preserve, preserve for me, O Master of the World, this palm grove of memory in the desert of my affliction. Defile not this happy place with blood. Let not the trees that heard thee but yesterday call me Friend bow their heads beneath the wind of anguish: let not the threshold which I have crossed blossom out with blood! Spare me, spare me from hearing that which will haunt me for ever and for ever – the moan of that white woman!

CALIPH (*to* GUARDS): Do not release him till the end. See that he keeps his eyes well opened, and feasts them to the fill.

(*Exit* CALIPH *and train.*)

(*The song of the* MUEZZIN *is heard,* '*La Allah illa Allah,*' *etc.*)

HASSAN: The sun has set. Guards, O Guards! (*No answer.*) It is the hour of prayer, do you not pray? I have still a little treasure. (*No answer from the* GUARDS.) Are you dumb? (GUARDS *nod.*) But why are you not deaf? (GUARDS *point to their tongues.*) Ah – your tongues have been torn out! (GUARD *points to window of the pavilion.*) What do you point at? ... Ah, Yasmin!

YASMIN: I have seen and heard behind the lattice. Hassan has fallen from power and favour.

HASSAN (*crazily*): Ah, good, very good, surpassing good! You are at the window – I am in the street. This is a reflection of that. As swans go double in a river, so do events come drifting down our lives. Again, again!

Bow down thy head, O burning bright! for one night or the other night
Will come the Gardener in white, and gathered flowers are dead, Yasmin!

Come now, a sweet lie first, Yasmin: sing a little how you love me. Show me your beauty limb by limb – then bring, ah, bring your new lover – mock my moon-touched verses and call me the fool, the old fool, the weary fool I am!

YASMIN: I will not yet call Hassan a fool. Hassan has fallen from power, but he need not fall from riches. The Palace Confectioner, Hassan, may still become the richest merchant in Bagdad.

HASSAN: Thou harlot, thou harlot, thou harlot!

YASMIN: Why art thou angry? In what have I insulted thee?

HASSAN: Oh, if it were thou about to suffer! If it were thou!

YASMIN (*staring across the garden and forgetting* HASSAN): At last, at last! – the Procession of Protracted Death! I shall see it all!

(*A deep red afterglow illumines the back of the garden. Across the garden towards the door of the pavilion moves in black silhouettes the Procession of Protracted Death, of which the order is this:*

MASRUR, *naked, with his scimitar.*

Four assistant torturers in black holding steel implements.

Two men in armour bearing a lighted brazier slung between them on a pole.

Two men bearing a monstrous wheel.

Four men carrying the rack.

A man with a hammer and a whip.

PERVANEH *and* RAFI, *half naked, pulling a cart that bears their coffins: their legs drag great chains.*

Behind each of them walks a soldier with uplifted sword. MASRUR *knocks at the door of the Pavilion: the* SLAVES *open and flee in terror at the sight. The light of the brazier glows through the windows. The* SOLDIERS *who guard* PERVANEH *and* RAFI *unhook the chains that chain them to the cart, and placing their hands on the necks of the prisoners push them in. The four* SLAVES *of the house then appear under the guidance of the man with the whip and lift in the coffins. Lastly,* HASSAN *is taken by his two* GUARDS *and forced to enter. The stage grows absolutely dark, save for the shining of the light from the windows. In the silence rises the splashing of the fountain and the whirring and whirling of a wheel. The sounds blend and grow unendurably insistent, and with them music begins to play softly. A cry of pain is half smothered by the violins. At last the silver light of the moon floods the garden.* HASSAN, *thrust forth by his* GUARDS, *appears at the door of the pavilion. His face is white and haggard: he totters a few steps and finally falls in a faint in the shadow of the fountain. The coffins are brought out, nailed down, and placed in the cart. The* SOLDIERS *pull the cart in place of the prisoners, and what remains of the procession departs in reverse order.* MASRUR *only has lingered by the door.* YASMIN *is clutching at his arm.*)

YASMIN: Masrur – thou dark Masrur!

MASRUR: Allah – the woman!

YASMIN: How you smell of blood!

MASRUR: And you of roses.

YASMIN: I laughed to see them writhe – I laughed, I laughed, as I watched behind the curtain. Why did you drink his veins?

MASRUR: A vow.

YASMIN: Will you not drink mine also?

MASRUR: Shall I put my arms around you?

YASMIN: Your arms are walls of black and shining stone. Your breast is the castle of the night.

MASRUR: Little white moth, I will crush you to my heart.

YASMIN (*with a sudden cry of terror, struggling from his embrace a moment after*): Ah, let me go. Do you hear them? ... Do you hear them? ...

MASRUR: What is there to hear but the noises of the night?

YASMIN (*springing away*): The flowers are talking ... the garden is alive. ... (*She falls.*)

MASRUR (*stooping to carry her*): She loves blood and is frightened of the moon. She is smooth and white. I will take her home.

(*Enter* ISHAK *searching for* HASSAN.)

ISHAK: Hassan – where doth he lie? Hassan, O Hassan. Thou hast broken that gentle heart, Haroun, and I have broken my lute: I play no more for thee. Ah, why did they not tell me sooner – I fear his reason may have fled before I find him: he may be wandering in the streets to-night like Death, and tearing at his eyes. Hassan, oh, Hassan!

It is he: he lies just as I first saw him: beneath a fountain, face toward the moon. His life is rhyming like a song: it harks back to the old refrain. Is life a mirror wherein events show double?

HASSAN (*half waking from his swoon*): Swans that drift into the mist. ...

ISHAK (*bending over him to raise him*): Friend, I am glad to hear thy voice. Rise, rise, thou art in a pitiable case.

HASSAN (*faintly*): Let me lie. ... This place is quiet, and the earth smells cool. May I never rise till they lift me aboard my coffin, and I'll go a sailing down the river and out to sea.

ISHAK: You are alive – no one will hurt you: hold to your reason and fight despair.

HASSAN: And in that sea are no red fish. ...

ISHAK: Come: rise: be brave: I know you have suffered.

HASSAN: She was brave. Ah, her hands, her hands!

ISHAK: Do not tell me that tale.

HASSAN: You are a poet. They cut off her lover's head and poured the blood upon her eyes!

ISHAK: Be silent. You are full of devils. I tell you, it is not true. Stop dreaming: look into my eyes: listen!

(*Bells are heard without the garden.*)

You hear? The camels are being driven to the Gate of the Moon. At midnight starts the great summer caravan for the cities of the Far North East, divine Bokhara and happy Samarkand. It is a desert path as yellow as the bright sea-shore: therefore the Pilgrims call it The Golden Journey.

HASSAN: And what of that to you or me, your Golden Journey to Samarkand?

ISHAK: I am leaving this city of slaves, this Bagdad of fornication. I have broken my lute and will write no more qasidahs in praise of the generosity of kings. I will try the barren road, and listen for the voice of the emptiness of earth. And you shall walk beside me.

HASSAN: I?

ISHAK: Rise, and confide to me once more the direction of your way.

HASSAN (*rising with* ISHAK'*s aid*): Why save me from a death desired? What am I to you or to any man living? Why would you force me like a fate to live?

ISHAK: Because I am your friend, and need you.

HASSAN: Oh, Ishak, singer of songs!

ISHAK: Prepare for travel.

HASSAN: I have no possessions.

ISHAK: O pilgrim! O true pilgrim! I have dinars of gold: we will furnish ourselves at the gate, and change these silks of indolence for the camel-hair of toil. But have you not one thing in your house to take – not one single thing?

HASSAN (*with a great shudder*): Within that door – nothing. But I have one old carpet that still lies in my shop. Its gentle flowers the negro has not defiled. And yet I dare not seek it.

ISHAK: I will bring it you. You shall stretch it out upon the desert when you say your evening prayer, and it shall be a little meadow in the waste of sand.

HASSAN (*seizing* ISHAK *in a sudden panic*): Keep close to me: do not leave me! The night is growing wild!

ISHAK: Hold to your reason! It is all stars and moon and crystal peace.

HASSAN: The trees are moving without a wind ... the flowers are talking ... the stars are growing bigger. ...

ISHAK: Be calm, there is nothing.

(*The fountain runs red.*)

116

HASSAN: The fountain – the fountain!

ISHAK: Oh! alas! it is pouring blood! Come away.

HASSAN: The Garden is alive!

ISHAK: Come away: it is haunted! Come away: come away! Follow the bells!

(*Exeunt in terror.*)

(*The* GHOST *of the Artist of the Fountain rises from the fountain itself in pale Byzantine robes.*)

FOUNTAIN GHOST: The garden to the ghosts. Come forth, new brother and new sister. Come forth while enough of earth's heavy influence remains upon you – to speak and to be seen. Come forth, and those who are past shall dance with those that are to come.

GHOST OF RAFI (*with the voice of* RAFI, *the clothes of* RAFI, *the broken fetters of* RAFI, *but pale ... as death*): We are here, O Shadow of the Fountain.

FOUNTAIN GHOST: Welcome, thou and thy white lady to these ... haunts. Wander at will. I have scared away the sons of flesh.

GHOST OF RAFI: How were they scared, those two?

FOUNTAIN GHOST: When the water turned from white to red their faces turned from red to white. They ran!

GHOST HIDDEN IN THE TREES: Ha! ha!

GHOST OF PERVANEH: Tell us, O Man of the Fountain, what shall we do?

FOUNTAIN GHOST: Nothing: you are dead.

GHOST OF PERVANEH: Shall we stay in this garden and be lovers still, and fly in the air and flit among the leaves?

FOUNTAIN GHOST: As long as you remember what you suffered, you will stay near the house where your blood was shed.

GHOST OF PERVANEH: We will remember that ten thousand years.

117

FOUNTAIN GHOST: You have forgotten you are a Spirit. The memories of the dead are thinner than their dreams.

GHOST OF PERVANEH: But you stay here, by the fountain.

FOUNTAIN GHOST: I created this fountain: what have you created in the world?

GHOST OF PERVANEH: Nothing but the story of our lives.

FOUNTAIN GHOST: That will not save you. You were spiritual even in life. I see it by the great shadows of your eyes. But I cared only for the earth. I loved the veins of the leaves, the shapes of crawling beasts, the puddle in the road, the feel of wood and stone. I knew the shapes of things so well that my sculpture was the best in all the world. Therefore my spirit is still heavy with memories of earth and I stay in the world I love. Do I desire to see the back of the moon?

GHOST OF PERVANEH: May not we stay also? May I not touch the shadow of his lips and hear the whisper of his love? Shall we be driven from here, O Man of the Fountain?

FOUNTAIN GHOST: How do I know? Can I foresee?

GHOST OF PERVANEH: Thou, too, dost not foresee. But what of Paradise, what of Infinity – what of the stars, and what of us?

FOUNTAIN GHOST: I know no more than you.

GHOST OF PERVANEH: Is the secret secret still, and this existence darker than the last?

FOUNTAIN GHOST: Didst thou hope for a revelation? Why should the dead be wiser than the living? The dead know only this – that it was better to be alive.

GHOST OF PERVANEH: But we shall feel no more pain – Oh, no more pain, Rafi!

118

FOUNTAIN GHOST: But you will feel so cold.

GHOST OF PERVANEH: With the fire of love within us?

FOUNTAIN GHOST: You will forget when the wind blows.

GHOST OF PERVANEH: Forget! Rafi, Rafi, shall we forget, Rafi?

GHOST OF RAFI (*in a thin voice like an echo*): Forget ... Rafi ...

FOUNTAIN GHOST: You will forget, when the great wind blows you asunder and you are borne on with ten million others like drops on a wave of air.

GHOST OF PERVANEH: There is a faith in me that tells me I shall not forget my lover though God forget the world. And where shall the wind take us?

FOUNTAIN GHOST: What do I know, or they? I only know it rushes.

GHOST OF PERVANEH: How do you know about the wind?

FOUNTAIN GHOST: Because it blows through the garden and drives the souls together.

GHOST OF PERVANEH: What souls?

FOUNTAIN GHOST: The souls of the unborn children that live in the flowers.

GHOST OF PERVANEH: And how do you know about the passage of ten million souls?

FOUNTAIN GHOST: They pass like a comet across the midnight skies.

GHOST OF PERVANEH: Phantoms shall not make me fear. But what of Justice and Punishment and Reason and Desire? What of the Lover in the Garden of Peace?

FOUNTAIN GHOST: Ask of the wind.

GHOST OF PERVANEH: I shall be answered: I know that in the end I shall find the Lover in the Garden of Peace.

VOICES: And what of Life?

GHOST OF PERVANEH: Who asks, What of Life?

FOUNTAIN GHOST: The spirits of those who will soon be born.

VOICES: We have left our flowers. We know we shall soon be born. What of Life, O dead?

GHOST OF PERVANEH (*with a great cry*): Why, Life ... is sweet, my children!

> (*The leaves of the trees begin to rustle.*)

FOUNTAIN GHOST: Listen to the trees.

GHOST OF PERVANEH: Is it coming?

FOUNTAIN GHOST: It is the wind. I must go down into the earth.

> (*The* FOUNTAIN GHOST *vanishes.*)

GHOST OF PERVANEH: Ah, I am cold – I am cold – beloved!

GHOST OF RAFI (*scarce visible and very faint*): Cold ... cold.

GHOST OF PERVANEH: Speak to me, speak to me, Rafi.

GHOST OF RAFI: Rafi – Rafi – who was Rafi?

GHOST OF PERVANEH: Speak to thy love – thy love – thy love.

GHOST OF RAFI: Cold ... cold ... cold.

(*The wind sweeps the* GHOSTS *out of the garden, seeming also to ring more wildly the bells of the Caravan.*)

SCENE II

At the Gate of the Moon, Bagdad. Blazing moonlight. MERCHANTS, CAMEL-DRIVERS *and their beasts,* PILGRIMS, JEWS, WOMEN, *all manner of people. By the barred gate stands the* WATCHMAN *with a great key. Among the pilgrims* HASSAN *and* ISHAK *in the robes of pilgrims.*

THE MERCHANTS (*together*):
　　Away, for we are ready to a man!
　　　　Our camels sniff the evening and are glad.
　　Lead on, O Master of the Caravan,
　　　　Lead on the Merchant-Princes of Bagdad.
THE CHIEF DRAPER:
　　Have we not Indian carpets dark as wine,
　　　　Turbans and sashes, gowns and bows and veils,
　　And broideries of intricate design,
　　　　And printed hangings in enormous bales?
THE CHIEF GROCER:
　　We have rose-candy, we have spikenard,
　　　　Mastic and terebinth and oil and spice,
　　And such sweet jams meticulously jarred
　　　　As God's Own Prophet eats in Paradise.
THE PRINCIPAL JEWS:
　　And we have manuscripts in peacock styles
　　　　By Ali of Damascus: we have swords
　　Engraved with storks and apes and crocodiles,
　　　　And heavy beaten necklaces for lords.
THE MASTER OF THE CARAVAN:
　　But you are nothing but a lot of Jews.
PRINCIPAL JEW:
　　Sir, even dogs have daylight, and we pay.
MASTER OF THE CARAVAN:
　　But who are ye in rags and rotten shoes,
　　　　You dirty-bearded, blocking up the way?
ISHAK:
　　We are the Pilgrims, master; we shall go
　　　　Always a little further: it may be
　　Beyond that last blue mountain barred with snow
　　　　Across that angry or that glimmering sea,

　　White on a throne or guarded in a cave

121

There lies a prophet who can understand
Why men were born: but surely we are brave,
Who take the Golden Road to Samarkand.

THE CHIEF MERCHANT:

We gnaw the nail of hurry. Master, away!

ONE OF THE WOMEN:

O turn your eyes to where your children stand.
Is not Bagdad the beautiful? O, stay!

MERCHANTS (*in chorus*):

We take the Golden Road to Samarkand.

AN OLD MAN:

Have you not girls and garlands in your homes?
Eunuchs and Syrian boys at your command?
Seek not excess: God hateth him who roams!

MERCHANTS (*in chorus*):

We take the Golden Road to Samarkand.

HASSAN:

Sweet to ride forth at evening from the wells,
When shadows pass gigantic on the sand,
And softly through the silence beat the bells
Along the Golden Road to Samarkand.

ISHAK:

We travel not for trafficking alone;
By hotter winds our fiery hearts are fanned:
For lust of knowing what should not be known,
We take the Golden Road to Samarkand.

MASTER OF THE CARAVAN:

Open the gate, O watchman of the night!

THE WATCHMAN:

Ho, travellers, I open. For what land
Leave you the dim-moon city of delight?

MERCHANTS (*with a shout*):

We take the Golden Road to Samarkand!

(*The Caravan passes through the gate.*)

WATCHMAN (*consoling the women*):
 What would ye, ladies? It was ever thus.
  Men are unwise and curiously planned.

A WOMAN:
 They have their dreams, and do not think of us.
  (*The WATCHMAN closes the gate.*)

VOICES OF THE CARAVAN (*in the distance singing*):
 We take the Golden Road to Samarkand.

CURTAIN

★

THE END

On the King Penguin Series, Clive Bell makes the following comment in the *New Statesman:* 'As the world grows poorer, stupider and worse educated, the chance of civilization surviving grows less. One begins to clutch at straws; and here, unexpectedly, comes floating by a plank. If the Penguin publishers really intend to issue a series of short, readable, illustrated monographs edited and written by scholars and people of taste, it is just possible they will arouse such interest in visual art that when that government comes into power which is to decree the conversion of all picture-galleries and museums to movie-houses, there will be quite a brisk opposition.'

WOOD ENGRAVINGS OF THOMAS BEWICK (K30)
John Rayner

65 reproductions of Bewick's wood engravings of birds, quadrupeds and country scenes with introductory text by John Rayner.

RUSSIAN ICONS (K33)
David Talbot Rice

16 colour plates of famous icons from the eleventh to the seventeenth century, with a text by the Professor of the History of Fine Art at Edinburgh University.

THE ENGLISH TRADITION IN DESIGN (K34)
John Gloag

The writer of the text has himself done much to promote good modern design, and the 72 plates of furniture, metal work, textiles, pottery, glass, illustrate the evolution of design from the Middle Ages to the present day.

SPIDERS (K35)
W. S. Bristowe

W. S. Bristowe, one of the most distinguished spider experts in the world, has written this book of fascinating stories about the much-maligned tribe of spiders; it has colour plates from so far unpublished Blackwell drawings.

THE LEAVES OF SOUTHWELL (K17)
N. Pevsner and F. Attenborough

32 plates illustrating the carvings of the Cathedral at Southwell photographed by F. L. Attenborough, with a 72-page introductory essay by Dr. Pevsner, Lecturer in Art at Birkbeck College, University of London.

THE MICROCOSM OF LONDON (K9)
John Summerson

16 colour plates from Rowlandson and Pugin's famous panorama of Regency London with a text by John Summerson, Curator of the Soane Museum.

WILD FLOWERS OF THE CHALK (K37)
John Gilmour

The text is by the Director of the Royal Horticultural Society's Wisley Gardens. The plates were specially painted by Irene Hawkins.

THE BAYEUX TAPESTRY (K10)
Sir Eric Maclagan

A complete record of the tapestry in colour and black and white, with an explanatory and critical monograph by Sir Eric Maclagan.

A PELICAN SELECTION

Two books which have been especially commissioned for the Pelican Series will be warmly welcomed by all those interested in the Theatre. Now that the outlook for the English Theatre is at last brightening again by the exemption of non-profit-making companies from entertainment tax, by the granting of a Charter to the Arts Council, and by the great resurgence of acting in the grand manner, these two books will have a particular interest.

A SHORT HISTORY OF ENGLISH DRAMA
B. Ifor Evans
A Pelican Book (A172) 1s. 6d.

Readers of Dr Evans's *Short History of English Literature* will know what to expect from this companion volume: a startling number of facts assembled in a very short book. The whole sweep of English drama is shown here from the miming 'joculator' of the early middle ages to Noel Coward and J. B. Priestley in our own day.

INTRODUCING SHAKESPEARE
G. B. Harrison
A Pelican Book (A43) 1s. 6d.

This is a third reprinting of one of the most popular Pelican Books so far issued. Dr Harrison is an expert on Elizabethan and Jacobean times. In *Introducing Shakespeare* he examines the story with fresh insight and curiosity.

Reprinting
LIFE IN SHAKESPEARE'S ENGLAND (A143)
J. Dover Wilson

Forthcoming
PRINCIPLES OF SHAKESPEAREAN PRODUCTION
G. Wilson Knight

FORD MADOX FORD

—

In every generation there appear authors who fail to secure in their life time the full reputation they deserve. One such was Ford Madox Ford who, when he died in 1939, had written about 70 books without ever, so to speak, getting his name in neon lights. It was partly his own fault, no doubt, for some of his books were casual and ephemeral. He was a copious and ardent writer and, apart from the creative work he accomplished in poetry, criticism and fiction, he founded *The English Review*, in whose pages many of the best English modern writers made their first appearance. As a novelist Ford Madox Ford never enjoyed a resounding popular success in this country, but he excited the admiration and respect of his fellow-novelists. In this sense he was a 'writer's writer,' and those who read the four novels of his now republished as Penguins will discover for themselves the scrupulous quality of his craftsmanship. He was not content, as many successful novelists are, to knock a story together, and in these novels the careful reader will discern the powerful and meticulous sense of structure which distinguished Ford Madox Ford's best work.

The four novels selected by Penguins to reveal this fine writer to a new generation are the Tietjens tetralogy (named after the central character) – *Some Do Not* (632), *No More Parades* (639), *A Man Could Stand Up* (640) – and *Last Post* (641). In each volume of this selected quartette there is printed a long essay on Ford Madox Ford specially written for the Penguin edition by R. A. Scott James, the well-known literary critic and an old personal friend of the novelist.

THE
PENGUIN MODERN PAINTERS

EDITED BY SIR KENNETH CLARK

—

The following titles are available in this series

two shillings and sixpence
†*three shillings and sixpence*

—

In preparation for future publication

A NEW VENTURE

—

One of the problems which beset the present-day publisher is the inability to bring before the reading public the increasing number of new books and new authors. The problem, created by lack of materials and skilled labour, is not mitigated by the fact that many famous modern books have gone out of print. It is almost certain that this is the first time in the history of publishing that such a position has arisen, but, serious as it is, the consequence is beneficial to the readers of Penguin Books.

Under an agreement which has been made between Penguin Books and five leading publishers – Chatto & Windus, Faber & Faber, Hamish Hamilton, Heinemann, and Michael Joseph – Penguins have the opportunity of reprinting some of these books, many by authors who have not appeared in Penguins before. The first ten titles were published in July, 1948, and a list of the second ten, of which the present volume is one, together with the previous publishers, is given below.

Hotel Splendide *by Ludwig Bemelmans* from Hamish Hamilton

The Sailor's Return and Beany-Eye *by David Garnett* from Chatto & Windus

Looking for a Blue-Bird *by Joseph Wechsberg* from Michael Joseph

No Bed for Bacon *by Caryl Brahms and S. J. Simon* from Michael Joseph

Music Ho! *by Constant Lambert* from Faber & Faber

Hassan *by James Elroy Flecker* from Heinemann

The Journal of a Disappointed Man *by W. N. P. Barbellion* from Chatto & Windus

The Smith of Smiths *by Hesketh Pearson* from Hamish Hamilton

Sherston's Progress *by Siegfried Sassoon* from Faber & Faber

Sons and Lovers *by D. H. Lawrence* from Heinemann

THE AUTHOR

THE life of James Elroy Flecker was a battle against ill-health. But no one shall say that it was a losing battle, since in spite of it, at the end of his fast declining years, he produced the masterpiece *Hassan*, with its colour and its wit and its passion, its alternation of merriment and of tragedy, and the strange beauty of its rhythms.

He was born in 1884 and was educated at Dean Close School, Cheltenham, Uppingham, and Trinity College, Oxford. Later he studied oriental languages at Caius, Cambridge, and joined the Consular Service in Constantinople in 1910. He fell ill; but, apparently quite recovered, he returned to Smyrna and married a Greek lady in Athens.

It was while in Corfu between June and August, 1911, while he was working for a Consular examination in Turkish, that he came upon an old Turkish farce about a credulous old man named Hassan whose friends delighted in playing practical jokes upon him.

Two years later, at Leysin in Switzerland, already in the grip of his malady, he began to write such a story in the light of his own inspiration. He barely won the race with death, which overtook him at Davos in 1915. For by then *Hassan* had just been finished. It was produced by Basil Dean at the Haymarket Theatre in London in 1923.

In person, Sir John Squire tells us, Flecker was tall, with blue eyes, straight hair and dark complexion. There was a tinge of the East in his appearance, and his habitual expression was a curious blend of the sardonic and the gentle.